Markt- und Unternehmensentwicklung
Markets and Organisations

Series Editors
Arnold Picot, München, Germany
Ralf Reichwald, Leipzig, Germany
Egon Franck, Zürich, Switzerland
Kathrin M. Möslein, Erlangen-Nürnberg, Germany

Change of institutions, technology and competition drives the interplay of markets and organisations. The scientific series 'Markets and Organisations' addresses a magnitude of related questions, presents theoretic and empirical findings and discusses related concepts and models.

More information about this series at http://www.springer.com/series/12561

Leontin Karl Grafmüller

Co-Creation of High-Tech Products in the B2B Domain

With a foreword by Prof. Dr. Kathrin M. Möslein

Springer Gabler

Leontin Karl Grafmüller
Leipzig, Germany

Dissertation HHL Leipzig Graduate School of Management, 2019

Markt- und Unternehmensentwicklung Markets and Organisations
ISBN 978-3-658-28411-4 ISBN 978-3-658-28412-1 (eBook)
https://doi.org/10.1007/978-3-658-28412-1

Springer Gabler

This Springer Gabler imprint is published by the registered company Springer Fachmedien Wiesbaden GmbH part of Springer Nature.
The registered company address is: Abraham-Lincoln-Str. 46, 65189 Wiesbaden, Germany

Foreword

More and more companies involve customers into the development of new products in order to enhance the likelihood of product success in the marketplace. Referred to as customer co-creation, providers develop novel offerings with their customers in a joint interaction process. While past research has mainly addressed the co-creation with consumers over the last two decades, the co-creation in the B2B context has been less in the focus of innovation research.

Considering the crucial role of business customers in the development of new offerings, Dr. Leontin Karl Grafmüller has well spotted the current need to better understand how B2B companies manage co-creation. He addresses this challenge within the B2B high-tech domain, building on and extending earlier works in the field.

His exploratory journey invites the reader to discover answers relating to

- promising practices for co-creation in the high-tech domain from the provider's perspective,
- business customers' value within the co-creation process, and
- a toolkit design for the co-creation of high-tech products, set up and tested with real-life data from a high-tech company.

The three empirical studies in this book tackle major challenges related to high product complexity in the co-creation process with business customers such as the time intensity or incorrect product specifications. With its exploratory approach, the thesis sheds light on actual practices, striking insights and promising opportunities for researchers and practitioners. The research at hand benefits from rich and thick qualitative research data, all gathered by the author, and convinces with its comprehensive presentation. Especially, the thesis appeals by its threefold focus on three vital research questions related to the co-creation of high-tech products in the B2B domain and its practical usefulness of the implications for managers.

In 2019, Leontin Karl Grafmüller's thesis has been accepted as doctoral dissertation at HHL Leipzig Graduate School of Management. The work appeals by its highly relevant focus, its clear line of argumentation and the didactic brilliance by which the research and findings are presented. As the book yields promising and convincing results, I highly recommend it to both innovation researchers and managers. I wish the book the attention and reception that it deserves – and Leontin only the best for his career.

Prof. Dr. Kathrin M. Möslein

Preface

This book focuses on the co-creation of high-tech products in the B2B domain and provides insights on the topic from different angles. As the complexity of products is constantly increasing and as customers are more deeply involved in co-creation, the book at hand deals with a visibly relevant topic in the context of open innovation. In this vein, companies use external resources such as customers to enhance their innovation activities, for which co-creation represents one powerful means. I seek to answer urgent questions concerning co-creating high-tech products in the industrial domain. More precisely, the three empirical studies deal with promising practices to face high product complexity in co-creation from the provider's perspective, customer perceived value within the co-creation process and opportunities to leverage toolkit opportunities in the early phase of co-creation.

Before diving deeper, I would like to express my profound thanks to my doctoral supervisor *Professor Kathrin M. Möslein* for her extraordinary support and continuous motivation. Kathrin, when we started narrowing down the topic, we experienced our very own "fuzzy front end". Especially at the beginning of this research project, you and *Dr. Hagen Habicht* were an endless source of motivation and optimism. For supporting me later in the process regarding journal publications, sincere thanks go to *Professor Vivek Velamuri* for constantly pushing me. Without you, Vivek, I would have been likely to lose my breath. Also, I would like to express my deepest thanks to *Professor Iris Hausladen* for the secondary supervision of my thesis.

The second part of my acknowledgements is dedicated to the CLIC team as well as the team from the Chair of Information Systems – Innovation & Value Creation at the Friedrich-Alexander University Erlangen-Nürnberg for supporting me. Dear *Dr. Claudia Lehmann,* you were a perfect manager to me, giving me exactly the right balance between freedom and duties. Also, *Dr. Marc Marheineke, Tim Mosig, Bettina Adler, Hannah Rein* and *Paula Rassmann* are to thank for being both supportive as well as competent colleagues and friends. I particularly thank my "research tandem" *Susanne*

Table of contents

Figures

Tables

Abbreviations

BMBF	Bundesministerium für Bildung und Forschung (translated from German: Federal Ministry of Education and Research)
B2B	business-to-business
B2C	business-to-consumer
CEO	Chief Executive Officer
cf.	confer
DSR	Design Science Research
e. g.	Latin: exempli gratia; for example
ETO	engineer-to-order
et al.	et alii
etc.	et cetera
FKZ	Förderkennzeichen (translated from German: funding code)
i. e.	Latin: id est; that is to say
ibid.	Latin: ibīdem; in the same place
p.	page
R&D	research & development
RQ	research question
SME	small and medium-sized enterprise
QDA	qualitative data analysis
Q	question

Part I – Introduction

L. K. Grafmüller, *Co-Creation of High-Tech Products in the B2B Domain*,
Markt- und Unternehmensentwicklung Markets and Organisations,
https://doi.org/10.1007/978-3-658-28412-1_1

1 Motivation of the research[1]

"We all struggle to co-create high-tech products with our customers. It is a mammoth task because products need so much intense explanation. But we must find ways to increase efficiency somehow." [2]

- Prof. Dr. Holger Erth, CEO of *Textilausrüstung Pfand GmbH*

Creating and designing products together with customers is not a new phenomenon in innovation research. Already in the early 1970s, researchers such as Nigel Cross have called for major rethinking and more customer integration in product design processes. Formerly discussed as *participatory design* (Cross, 1972), it has gained heavy interest almost half a century later in both innovation research and practice referred to as *customer co-creation*[3] (Gemser & Perks, 2015; Mustak, Jaakkola, & Halinen, 2013; Piller, Ihl, & Vossen, 2010; Prahalad & Ramaswamy, 2004a). In the paradigm of *open innovation* (Reichwald & Piller, 2006; Teplov, Albats, & Podmetina, 2018; von Hippel, 2005a), customers take an active role in product development processes. This constitutes a strong contrast to traditional market research approaches fully under the control of the company (Piller et al., 2012). Not only developers, engineers or other stakeholders from the organization are involved in product development, but also customers contribute to the development in their role as *co-creators* (Prahalad & Ramaswamy, 2004b). Customers themselves are at the centre of co-creation, given a voice to articulate their needs in the midst of development processes (Prahalad & Ramaswamy, 2004b).

One major advantage of co-creation is that it reduces the risk associated with product launches (Cui & Wu, 2017; Hoyer, Chandy, Dorotic, Krafft, & Singh, 2010; Prahalad & Ramaswamy, 2002), as new products often fall below expectations. In numbers, more than 50% of new products fail in the market, as Cooper (2008) suggests. Other scholars,

---

[1] The first part of the motivation follows a book chapter by Grafmüller and Möslein (2017); all publications of the author of this dissertation are listed in *Annex I*.

[2] This quote represents an excerpt of an interview conducted by the author of this dissertation.

[3] In favor of better legibility, this research uses the abbreviated form *co-creation* in order to refer to *customer co-creation*. This is in line with a series of other studies, e. g. Beutel, Jonas, and Möslein (2017), Gemser and Perks (2015), Piller, Vossen, and Ihl (2012).

for instance Harvard Business School Professor Clay Christensen, estimate that even 95% of new products remain without success (Noble, 2011). Co-creation allows for increasing the likelihood of product success by involving customers into the product development, translating their needs directly into product designs (Sanders & Stappers, 2008; Witell, Kristensson, Gustafsson, & Löfgren, 2011). Further, Geyer, Lehnen, and Herstatt (2018) found in their recent study that joint development with customers is most useful for a company to identify customer requirements.

Bearing on the research area of co-creation, two publicly supported projects, as part of a large-scale research initiative, were dedicated to the B2B high-tech domain over the last four years[4]. This dissertation was carried out within these projects that have spanned across the entire B2B high-tech textile industry in Germany. More than 50 companies were involved in this research. The projects were arranged in a highly interdisciplinary way, formally encompassing a dozen partner organizations from research and practice. Collaboration was intense, as the tasks required constant exchange between the different partners to achieve shared understanding, to bridge the different fields of knowledge and to co-create the concepts that were later tested in practice. Targeting the co-creation of high-tech products from an innovation management research perspective, a couple of dozen company visits in 2015 served to get familiar with this high-tech textile industry. In doing so, the author had the opportunity to cautiously approach and learn about their business models, established practices, industry peculiarities and – much more compelling – the current hotspots of these B2B companies. And indeed, the companies stressed the co-creation of high-tech products as a major challenge because of the ever greater product complexity and increasing degrees of customer integration in innovation activities. Although this industry is acknowledged for being open, technologically innovative and transparent with their customers, the co-creation process was stressed as a major challenge throughout all the companies visited. The current co-creation activities were characterized by unstructured, trial-and-error and never-ending development projects as well as informally established practices.

[4] The German Federal Ministry of Education and Research (BMBF) funded two projects within the large-scale initiative *futureTEX* (FKZ: 03ZZ0604A; 03ZZ0618B). These two projects form the research context for this dissertation. This context of this research is deeper described in *Chapter 3* of *Part I*.

When visiting the companies, the company representatives in charge of co-creating high-tech products were usually struggling to delineate a typical co-creation process, because there were no formal structures in place. Neither were they able to describe the customer and his preferences to be involved in co-creation, but understanding the customer and his motivation is crucial to arrange the overall co-creation process (Frow, Nenonen, Payne, & Storbacka, 2015). Moreover, information systems remained widely unexploited with regard to supporting co-creation activities. Against this backdrop, the introductory quote can be considered exemplary: most of the companies have recognized that they need to tackle the topic of co-creation in a more structured and efficient way, and that they need to enhance co-creation processes with their customers. Hence, over the last four years, the goal has matured to understand this domain and to develop, test and especially evaluate possible solutions in this context of high-tech product co-creation. With regards to the challenging significance of the topic, it appears fruitful to raise the following question of interest: *how can companies better manage co-creation in the B2B high-tech domain?*

When reviewing extant research on the co-creation of high-tech products, it was a tough task to identify suitable approaches for this domain. Especially when dealing with high product complexity and the B2B context. And, moreover, a closer look at extant literature reveals that the co-creation of high-tech offerings represents a challenge across various disciplines: studies calling for further action were found in innovation management (e. g. Barczak, 2012; Biemans & Langerak, 2015; Gemser & Perks, 2015; Geyer et al., 2018; Wei, 2012), industrial marketing management (e. g. Aarikka-Stenroos & Jaakkola, 2012; La Rocca, Moscatelli, Perna, & Snehota, 2016) and service management (e. g. Nordin & Kowalkowski, 2010; Perks, Gruber, & Edvardsson, 2012). This entails to approach the question in an exploratory way.

The goal of this dissertation is to better understand co-creation with its established processes and underlying challenges in the B2B high-tech domain. Also, it aims at building an artefact to foster efficiency within a real-life setting. As theoretical lens, the dissertation takes a problem-solving perspective (Newell & Simon, 1972; von Hippel, 1994) as the co-creation process between customer and provider is often conceptualized as joint problem solving (e.g. Piller, Ihl, & Vossen, 2011; Prahalad & Ramaswamy,

2004b). According to the explorative nature of the question raised above, and as the literature is scarce on the co-creation of high-tech products in the B2B domain (e. g. Mustak et al., 2013), the overall dissertation is characterized by the qualitative research paradigm. This is particularly suitable when intricate, unknown phenomena are at the centre of interest (Mason, 2002, p. 3). Qualitative data for this dissertation is generated via interviews, focus groups as well as workshops; all conducted within the German high-tech textile industry from the B2B context.

After the motivation of this research, *Chapter 2* further exposes the literature with its theoretical perspective used in this dissertation and with particular interest for high-tech products and the B2B context. Based on that, research gaps in extant research are set out. *Chapter 3* presents the context of this research and showcases several product scenarios. Finally, *Chapter 4* provides the structure and sets out the three empirical parts of the dissertation.

2 Framing

Research emphasizes that a closer customer orientation reduces uncertainty for successful product launch (Achilladelis, Jervis, & Robertson, 1971; Cui & Wu, 2017; Levitt, 1960; Lin & Huang, 2013). Refined for decades, however, traditional market research with interviews or static surveys remains frequently below expectations (Witell et al., 2011)[5].

In his early work, an important downside is described in the *manufacturer-active paradigm*[6] for product idea generation by von Hippel (1978) who argues for several weaknesses: the manufacturer picks and surveys assumingly appropriate customer groups to obtain valuable data and develops a *"hopefully responsive product idea"* (ibid., p. 243) by translating customer needs into technical specifications and a product design. The new designs are then tested against customer perceptions in numerous iterations, typically with the usage of prototypes. In his early work, von Hippel (1978) frames the role of the customer in this paradigm to merely respond *"speaking only when spoken to"* (ibid., p. 243). In this vein of enhancing the success of new product development, the role of the customer has changed significantly over the last years: the customer has been recognized as an active participant in innovation activities (Gambardella, Raasch, & von Hippel, 2017). The customer himself is involved in innovation instead of just answering static survey questions. As a consequence, *co-creation* has prevailed in numerous domains as a form of *open innovation* and has yielded numerous studies in innovation research (e. g. Gemser & Perks, 2015; Piller, Möslein, Ihl, & Reichwald, 2017; Randhawa, Wilden, & Hohberger, 2016).

The subsequent *sections* give insight into this research field. First, the fundamentals of co-creation with special emphasis on conceptual clarity are presented. Second, a state of the art of the co-creation of high-tech products is set out for the B2B domain. Third,

[5] In their empirical study that compares co-creation with traditional market research techniques, Witell et al. (2011) denote co-creation as *proactive*, while traditional market research is *reactive*.

[6] The opposite pole for the *manufacturer-active paradigm* delineated by von Hippel (1978) is labeled *customer-active paradigm*, which Piller et al. (2010) and Bogers, Afuah, and Bastian (2010) consider an early precursor for the subsequent works in the area of *open innovation* and *co-creation*.

the theoretical perspective to examine the topic under investigation is depicted with a focus on the high-tech domain. Finally, three research gaps are exhibited based on extant literature.

2.1 Fundamentals of co-creation

This *section* depicts the fundamentals of co-creation for this dissertation. It encompasses a classification and definition of co-creation as well as a detailing on conceptual clarity.

Being a central topic in innovation management for more than 40 years (Cross, 1972; Lovelock & Young, 1979; Mustak et al., 2013; von Hippel, 1978), the participation of customers in the creation of offerings has spanned across various innovation research topics in the 21st century. Although discussed for a relatively long period, the context is continuously changing. This makes the topic a perennial issue in innovation research (Biemans & Langerak, 2015; Bstieler et al., 2018; Geyer et al., 2018; Teplov et al., 2018; Tidd & Bessant, 2018). Nowadays, customers participate in the creation of offerings in different ways. Keinz, Hienerth, and Lettl (2012) give three examples: *mass customization* with toolkits to achieve inexpensive product individualization (Gilmore & Pine, 1997; Piller, Möslein, & Stotko, 2004), *innovation contests* as a crowdsourcing approach where community members propose diverse solutions for a challenge prescribed by an organization (Haller, Bullinger, & Möslein, 2011; Howe, 2006) and *co-creation* with lead-users as a method to involve highly motivated customers directly into product development (von Hippel, 2005b). All of these topics unite the paradigm of *open innovation* (Reichwald & Piller, 2006), acknowledged for its close customer orientation (von Hippel, 2005b).

In this dissertation, *(customer) co-creation* is considered as one form of open innovation (Ihl & Piller, 2010; Prahalad & Ramaswamy, 2004a). The Latin prefix *co-* relates to the joint and mutual *creation* of something, indicating the relation between two subjects (Thallmaier, 2015, p. 11). The focus is on the integration of customers into the creation of new offerings (Gemser & Perks, 2015; Prahalad & Ramaswamy, 2004a;

Ramaswamy & Ozcan, 2018). The research at hand follows the definition for *(customer) co-creation* introduced by Piller et al. (2011, p. 31):

> *"Customer co-creation denotes an active, creative and social collaboration process between producers (retailers) and customers (users), facilitated by the company. Customers become active participants in an innovation process of a firm and take part in the development of new products or services."*

As indicated in the definition, co-creation is characterized by a high degree of interactivity between the customer and provider (Normann & Ramírez, 1993; Reichwald & Piller, 2006, p. 47). Further, it stresses the active role of the customer in the joint development of new offerings (Kleinaltenkamp, Bach, & Griese, 2009). Given that, Kleinaltenkamp et al. (2009) argue that co-creation is the next level of customer integration because the latter mainly stresses the provider perspective: co-creation puts the equality between customer and provider into focus. Despite of this equality, still the definition indicates the consensus that the provider is in charge of managing, organizing and taking precautions for a successful co-creation process (Frow et al., 2015; Malshe & Friend, 2018; Piller et al., 2012). Therefore, the proper conduct of co-creation is considered a management task in innovation research in order to ensure both its efficiency and efficacy (Galvagno & Dalli, 2014; Harmancioglu, McNally, Calantone, & Durmusoglu, 2007; Hienerth & Lettl, 2011). In this regard, the co-creation process is often stressed as decisive success factor (Frow et al., 2015; Malshe & Friend, 2018; Roberts, Hughes, & Kertbo, 2014).

Since also other research streams touch upon the term of co-creation, the following paragraphs are dedicated to conceptual clarity in this dissertation. This appears specifically requisite as several recent studies stress the need for conceptual clarity in co-creation research (Mustak et al., 2013; Ramaswamy & Ozcan, 2018). One scholar of the seminal works on the topic (Prahalad & Ramaswamy, 2000, 2004b), Venkat Ramaswamy, emphasizes the two major different, but intertwined streams in a recent article (Ramaswamy & Ozcan, 2018). It is called for a clear demarcation between the co-creation of value and offerings. To put it clearly, (customer) co-creation shall not be confused with value co-creation. The latter is postulated through the service lens of the service-dominant logic introduced by Vargo and Lusch (2004). In a recent literature review on the theory of value co-creation, Galvagno and Dalli (2014) define it as *"the joint, collaborative, concurrent, peer-like process of producing new value"* (ibid., p. 644). The difference between the two concepts is, obviously, that value co-creation aims at jointly creating value, while customer co-creation targets the joint development of a product or service (Galvagno & Dalli, 2014; Mustak et al., 2013).

However, several studies neglect in which of these areas they are grounded (e. g. Frow et al., 2015; Füller, Hutter, & Faullant, 2011). This makes it difficult to assess and use them, as emphasized by Mustak et al. (2013, p. 342):

> *"This has resulted in an apparent lack of conceptual clarity. It also seems that many authors use the term "co-creation" without specifying whether they refer to customer participation in the offering creation process, or customer participation in the value creation process."*

Nonetheless, this lack of conceptual clarity in extant research is not striking as the concepts are interwoven. For an overview, *Table 1* presents three commonalities between value co-creation and customer co-creation in order to argue for the relevance of studies from the value co-creation domain for this dissertation.

Table 1: Three commonalities between *value co-creation* and *customer co-creation*

Commonality	In value co-creation research	In customer co-creation research
Joint problem solving	Within the service-dominant logic, Aarikka-Stenroos and Jaakkola (2012) and Grönroos and Voima (2013) conceptualize *value co-creation* as a collaborative interaction process that targets joint problem solving.	Piller et al. (2010) depict *customer co-creation* as an intense customer-provider interaction and as directed problem-solving activities taking place within the innovation process.
High degree of knowledge exchange between customer and provider	By means of knowledge exchange between customer and provider, *value* is created (Ballantyne & Varey, 2006; Grönroos, 2004).	An intense knowledge exchange is the basis for the joint creation of an *offering* (Prahalad & Ramaswamy, 2004b).
	In contrastive studies on the two concepts	
Joint creation of *something*	Following Ramaswamy and Ozcan (2018), both concepts exhibit a high degree of interactivity with the goal of a joint creation of *something*. For theorization, it is termed as 'creation through interactions'. Also Galvagno and Dalli (2014) and Mustak et al. (2013) stress the creation of *something* in the fields of co-creation research, but with deviating goals.	

Based on these commonalities, it is argued that the concepts customer co-creation and value co-creation are distinct, but overlapping. This is why several studies in both research strands call for a reciprocal benefit of the intertwined fields (Grönroos & Ravald, 2011; Lusch, 2006; Mustak et al., 2013; Randhawa et al., 2016). As a consequence, this dissertation also builds on studies from the value co-creation domain. It follows recent recommendations from innovation research in order to yield richer insight (Mustak et al., 2013; Ramaswamy & Ozcan, 2018; Randhawa et al., 2016). In particular, Randhawa et al. (2016) advise to consider the wider business community for conducting innovation research, not only innovation-specific journals. They especially highlight the opportunities of benefitting from service-dominant logic studies for the enhancement of the research on customer co-creation because of the interrelation between the distinct concepts.

2.2 Co-creation in the high-tech B2B domain

This *section* showcases the state of the art in extant research on the co-creation in the high-tech B2B domain. It starts off with the classification of the term *high-tech product*, depicts the importance of co-creation for the high-tech B2B context and provides an overview of co-creation process aspects with special emphasis on *how* such processes are carried out.

In innovation research, a high-tech product is characterized by a high level of complexity (Madhavaram & Appan, 2010; Olausson & Berggren, 2010). Different fields of knowledge and skills as well as specialized knowledge are needed for their development (La Rocca et al., 2016; Olausson & Berggren, 2012; Simon, 1962). Further, the seminal work on complexity by Simon (1962) depicts the intricate interaction between the numerous components. Also more recent studies state that product complexity is specifically influenced by the number of components (Gosling & Naim, 2009; Haug, Ladeby, & Edwards, 2009; Novak & Eppinger, 2001). Compared to simple product development, Olausson and Berggren (2010) argue that high-tech product development is far more concerned of unpredictable changes, severe delays and cost overruns (see e. g. Nightingale, 2000). Regarding the costs, the development of high-tech products is expensive due to its iterative development, inclusion of numerous stakeholders and engineering cycles of the various components. Moreover, the development process is often associated with uncertainty perceived by the involved stakeholders due to the high complexity (La Rocca et al., 2016).

Looking at product archetypes, products with a high degree of complexity are often described in the literature as engineer-to-order (ETO). Most notably, ETO products include an engineering part to every product and to every customer (Gosling & Naim, 2009; Haug, Hvam, & Mortensen, 2013; Hicks, McGovern, & Earl, 2000). *Figure 1* allocates ETO to the archetypes of customized products and exhibits its degree of customer integration and product complexity. As shown, ETO represents the most complex product archetype, requiring the highest degree of customer integration.

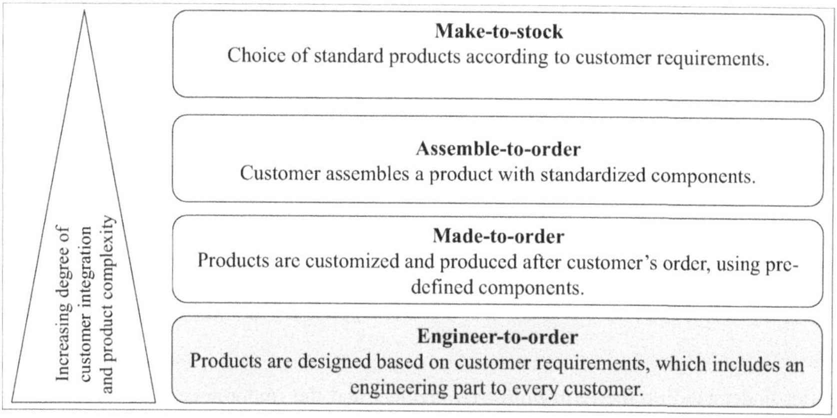

Figure 1: Product archetypes with degree of complexity and customer integration[7]

In ETO, the undefined solution space is a challenge due to the engineering part of every project. This means that ETO often complements a standard product with a non-predefined customization. This makes a joint development process mandatory between customer and provider to capture the requirements in a joint problem solving process, as La Rocca et al. (2016, p. 46) state:

> *"Interaction is needed because the complex offering solutions cannot first be conceived and developed and then implemented; they must be 'enacted jointly' between the user/customer and producer/supplier organizations."*[8]

ETO, as the term suggests, entails an intense co-creation between customer and provider. However, due to the high complexity, the overall buying as well as the joint design process are time bottlenecks for ETO (Gosling & Naim, 2009). This indicates the potential lack of efficiency in such development projects. But also the efficacy is challenging: it is decisive to capture customer's requirements properly within the co-creation process, as this forms the basis for a successful product design (Engelbrektsson &

[7] Illustration is based on Piller et al. (2004); descriptions follow Mihiotis (2014); Olhager (2003).
[8] Emphasis adopted by the authors La Rocca et al. (2016).

Söderman, 2004). If there are wrong specifications, the development entails more time-consuming cycles, and runs into danger of cost overruns (Bare & Cox, 2008). Especially when customer requirements are unveiled lately, the entire concept is likely to require major revision (Ullman, 2010, p. 135). Also, the importance of a clear identification of customer's requirements is linked to pitfalls such as late concept revisions, corrections of the production respectively machines, and dissatisfaction of all parties involved (Cooper, 1999; Engelbrektsson & Söderman, 2004). This is why the elicitation of customer's requirements is particularly important in high-tech, innovative product development (La Rocca et al., 2016; Madhavaram & Appan, 2010).

After understanding the term *high-tech product* and the importance of co-creation in this respect, the following paragraphs focus on two topics discussed in the literature against this backdrop. On the one hand, the significant information asymmetry is depicted, and on the other hand, the question is raised whether to structure or not to structure such co-creation processes.

On the one hand, a significant information asymmetry is often stressed in the context of co-creating high-tech products (Aarikka-Stenroos & Jaakkola, 2012; Alejandro, Souza, Boles, Ribeiro, & Monteiro, 2011; Ghosh, Dutta, & Stremersch, 2006). This results in a strong dependence between the parties involved (Möller & Törrönen, 2003; Tuli, Kohli, & Bharadwaj, 2007). In order to bridge this gap, there is a strong need for explanation by the provider (Aarikka-Stenroos & Jaakkola, 2012; Fauska, Kryvinska, & Strauss, 2014; Johnsen & Ford, 2007; Tuli et al., 2007). One key challenge is, however, that the customer himself often has a limited understanding of his needs, which makes the process difficult and fuzzy (Lapierre, 1997; Nordin & Kowalkowski, 2010). Although the customer often has much more knowledge then he knows, given the fact that he is much more familiar with his business (Bettencourt, Ostrom, Brown, & Roundtree, 2002), it is the provider's task to elicit this knowledge.

On the other hand, the question is raised whether to structure or not to structure co-creation processes because of their fuzziness (Backman, Börjesson, & Setterberg, 2007), ambiguity (Brun, Steinar Saetre, & Gjelsvik, 2009) and non-linearity (La Rocca et al., 2016). Also, it is asked if it makes sense to structure them because this may reduce the desired flexibility of the process (Olausson & Berggren, 2010). In this regard, extant research has reached consensus that the benefits of management approaches, i. e. planning and (partial) formalization outweigh the negatives (La Rocca et al., 2016; Olausson & Berggren, 2010; Shenhar, 1998). Therefore, joint development processes need to be carried out in an organized and flexible way to increase efficacy and efficiency (Olausson & Berggren, 2010). An empirical study found hybrid approaches useful, combining rather formal approaches to handle key aspects with *"quasi-formalized"* ones in order to be able to flexibly adapt to the non-linear and dynamic nature of the processes (Olausson & Berggren, 2010, p. 395). Moreover, the management of high-tech product development is an increasingly urgent topic: for instance, Suh (2005, p. 11) considers the ever-greater complexity one of the most urgent scientific and technological challenges. Deeper knowledge intensiveness as well as technological complexity are constantly rising in numerous industries (Graevenitz, Wagner, & Harhoff, 2011; Jacob & Ulaga, 2008; La Rocca et al., 2016; Möller, 2006). Briefly, the development of high-tech products benefits from and needs innovation research efforts in favor of balancing structure and flexibility.

Having introduced the essentials of co-creating high-tech products, the literature is reviewed that deals with aspects on *how* co-creation processes are carried out. This lays the basis to better understand how companies successfully manage co-creation in the B2B high-tech domain. To start off, it is reasonable to state that the literature on co-creating high-tech products with business customers is rather scarce (Ghosh et al., 2006; La Rocca et al., 2016; Madhavaram & Appan, 2010; Mustak et al., 2013). In this vein, Ghosh et al. (2006) emphasize that related research has mainly been carried out in B2C environments. A recent study by Mustak et al. (2013) reinforces this point: it is unveiled that the participation of business customers at the creation of offerings has been widely unexplored. This article found that only nine out of 163 articles examine the participation of business customers at new product development (Mustak et al., 2013), expressed as follows in *Figure 2*. A number of studies argues that this is a considerable omission of research, when contemplating the important role of business customers in the creation of offerings (La Rocca et al., 2016; Malshe & Friend, 2018; Mustak et al., 2013; Vaquero Martín, Reinhardt, & Gurtner, 2016).

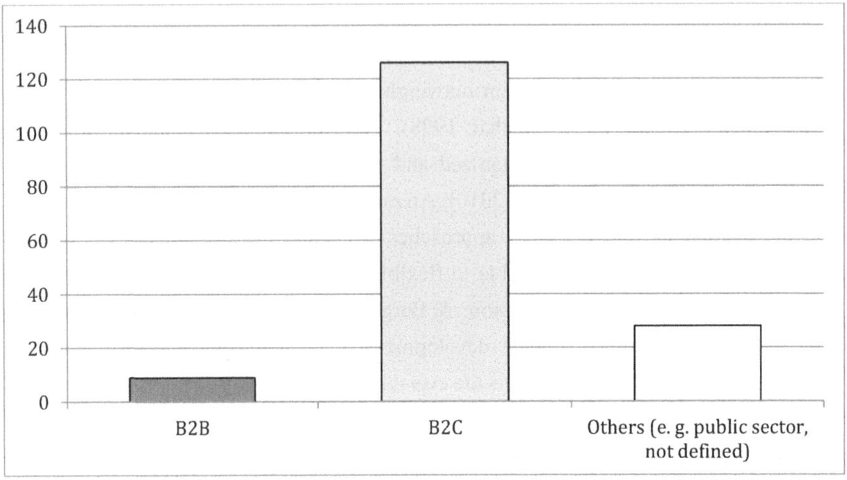

Figure 2: Distribution of studied domains in co-creation following Mustak et al. (2013)

Despite this shortcoming in extant research, an overview of the process aspects of co-creating high-tech products is provided in *Table 2* with special emphasis on *how* processes need to be managed. The following five aspects need to be taken into consideration when co-creating high-tech products, which are deeper depicted with description and statements from extant research in *Table 2*:

(1) Depth of customer integration

(2) Breadth of customer integration

(3) Stakeholder choice

(4) Mode of interaction

(5) Customer motivation

Table 2: Five aspects of the co-creation process in the high-tech B2B domain

Aspect with description	Statement from extant literature
(1) Depth of customer integration denotes the extent to which the customer is involved in co-creation (Fang, Palmatier, & Evans, 2008).	- Customers are deeply involved (La Rocca et al., 2016; Ogawa & Piller, 2006). - Interaction process is intense and degree of interaction very high (Hobday, 1998; Ogawa & Piller, 2006; Olausson & Berggren, 2010).
(2) Breadth of customer integration describes the period and timing of customer involvement into co-creation (Fang et al., 2008).	- An early involvement of customers is advised as this has the main impact (Koen et al., 2001; Witell et al., 2011) and because it avoids late modifications (Engelbrektsson & Söderman, 2004) - A deep involvement throughout the entire process is advised to ideally avoid wrong specifications (Aarikka-Stenroos & Jaakkola, 2012; La Rocca et al., 2016; Ogawa & Piller, 2006), *"not only early and late"* (Laage-Hellman, Lind, & Perna, 2014, p. 257).
(3) Stakeholder choice relates to the customers and company departments to be involved (Haas, Snehota, & Corsaro, 2012).	- Engineers and development managers typically handle complexity in high-tech development (Ulrich & Eppinger, 2012, p. 34). - Different expertises are needed instead of single actors, from various departments (i. e. also procurement, sales…) (Olausson & Berggren, 2012).
(4) Mode of interaction denotes which media are used in favor of co-creation, e. g. synchronous (face-to-face) vs. asynchronous (mail, telephone) (Aarikka-Stenroos & Jaakkola, 2012; Daft & Lengel, 1986).	- Face-to-face is best, because it decreases the perceived complexity by the customer (Aarikka-Stenroos & Jaakkola, 2012; Heide & John, 1990). - High-tech products require face-to-face because they need explanation, ideally done in person (Fauska et al., 2014; La Rocca et al., 2016). - The required interactive processes between customer and provider are hard to transfer to an asynchronous solution, i. e. to a toolkit (Fauska et al., 2014; Salomonson, Åberg, & Allwood, 2012). - Boundary objects are important because prototypes lower perceived complexity (Leonard-Barton, 1991) and because they support quick understanding (Wheelwright & Clark, 1994).
(5) Customer motivation describes what encourages customers to properly engage in the co-creation process (Mustak et al., 2013).	- The success of the co-creation process fundamentally relies on customer engagement (Hakanen & Jaakkola, 2012; Jaakkola & Alexander, 2014; La Rocca et al., 2016; Roberts et al., 2014). - Eggert and Ulaga (2002) describe that B2B customers *"buy for economic rather than emotional reasons"* (ibid., p. 109). - Although business customers are typically described to value speed, functional fit and efficiency (Gordon, Calantone, & Di Benedetto, 1993; Kumar & Grisaffe, 2004; Lapierre, 1997; Ulaga & Eggert, 2005), more recent studies indicate the importance of emotional and social value for the B2B context (Candi & Kahn, 2016; Prior, 2013).

2.3 Theoretical lens: The problem-solving perspective

Co-creation is conceptualized as a joint problem solving process between the customer and provider (e. g. Aarikka-Stenroos & Jaakkola, 2012; Piller et al., 2010; Prahalad & Ramaswamy, 2004a; Witell et al., 2011). Therefore, this dissertation uses the problem-solving perspective (Nickerson & Zenger, 2004; von Hippel, 1994) as a suitable theoretical lens to study co-creation. It starts off with an overview of the relevant works, which is then brought into context for this dissertation with its focus on the B2B high-tech domain.

Studies on problem solving date back to early theoretical works by Newell and Simon (1972) and Simon (1978), who do not focus on dyadic, but on individual problem solving. In Simon's (1978) information-processing theory of human problem solving, he describes problem solving as a ubiquitous human activity of search that ranges from highly structured to fuzzy and ill-structured tasks. While several tasks require only the description to be solved by humans, other tasks prerequisite several fields of expertise and in-depth knowledge. For such ill-structured tasks, Simon (1973) proposes that processes used to solve complex tasks follow a certain routine, when the problem solver can refer back to relevant long-term memory knowledge. A problem solver develops *"possible programs (strategies)"*[9] to face complexity evoked by ill-structured tasks (Simon, 1978, p. 273). In other words, the development of routines constitutes a means to master complex tasks.

The problem-solving perspective has regained attention within the knowledge-based view in the theory of the firm (Conner, 1991; Grant, 1996) and has experienced strong interest in research (Huang & Holden, 2016; Nickerson & Zenger, 2004). Particularly, the knowledge-based theory of the firm from Nickerson and Zenger (2004) has advanced the problem-solving perspective (see e. g. Felin & Zenger, 2014; Jeppesen & Lakhani, 2010; Lakhani, Lifshitz-Assaf, & Tushman, 2013). In sum, the problem-solving theory builds on the complexity theory by Simon (1962), transaction cost economics by Williamson (1981) and the knowledge-based view (Foss, 1996; Grant, 1996). The authors Nickerson and Zenger (2004) consider the firm as a problem-solving entity that

[9] Brackets are adopted by the original source by Simon (1978).

aims to identify and solve valuable problems. Moreover, by organizing problem-solving activities in an efficient and effective way, the company creates value. From this perspective, it is assumed that new knowledge is created by combining existing knowledge (Huang & Holden, 2016; Nickerson & Zenger, 2004), and it is the management's task to structure these processes. The critical question that Nickerson and Zenger (2004) address in their problem-centered knowledge-based theory is *"how a manager should organize individuals to generate knowledge that the firm seeks"* (ibid., p. 618).

A related topic in the context of problem solving constitutes the *stickiness* of information. Found in an early work by Polanyi (1966), the concept of stickiness is used to explain why some individuals seem to know more than they can explain (Polanyi, 1966). For discussing the *tacitness* or *stickiness* of information, it is often referred to the work of von Hippel (1994) in the context of innovation-related problem solving. He defines sticky information *"as the incremental expenditure required to transfer [a] unit of information to a specified locus in a form usable by a given information seeker"* (ibid., p. 423). The focus is on stickiness, and when costs of information transfer are low, stickiness is low, and vice versa. Here, sticky information is the part of information that one is not able to verbalize or articulate, which means that the information seeker aims to elicit this part of information in a way that he can use it, which can be costly. Von Hippel further depicts that central tendencies in economic theorizing have rather been characterized by a view of costless information transfer – but he argues that this is fundamentally different (von Hippel, 1994). He considers sticky information as the major reason why technical problem solving is costly to acquire and transfer to a new locus. Given this, it becomes more and more obvious why the problem-solving perspective, accompanied with the concept of sticky information, is often used as a theoretical foundation in the co-creation context in innovation research (Barczak, 2012; Gemser & Perks, 2015; Prahalad & Ramaswamy, 2004a; Vaquero Martín et al., 2016): co-creation brings problem solvers and problem seekers together for a joint development of a new offering in a close customer-provider interaction.

Taking a deeper look at co-creation from a problem-solving perspective, it is characterized by a rather ill-structured task because, typically, the information needed to solve the problem is not included in the problem description (Simon, 1973). It is rather the opposite: the problem itself needs to be defined as a part of the co-creation process (Prahalad & Ramaswamy, 2004b). The providing company is in charge of this problem definition and solving (Huang & Holden, 2016; Nickerson & Zenger, 2004), as it is consensus in co-creation (e. g. Aarikka-Stenroos & Jaakkola, 2012; Piller et al., 2010). Further, the problem-solving perspective on co-creation appears suitable because one major challenge is to bridge knowledge asymmetries to solve a problem by organizing problem-solving activities in an efficient and effective way (Nickerson & Zenger, 2004). In this context, co-creation can be conceptualized as one means for problem solving that needs to be structured and organized. Or, to put it in the context of the problem-solving perspective within the knowledge-based theory by Nickerson and Zenger (2004), co-creation represents an approach to *"organize individuals to generate knowledge that the firm seeks"* (ibid., p. 618). Thus, the customer brings in knowledge that the company desires.

Moving to the question what kind of knowledge the customer brings in via co-creation, the concept of sticky information by von Hippel (1994) is particularly helpful from a theoretical viewpoint. Most notably, the power of co-creation lies in its capacity to elicit sticky information from the customer in the joint development process (Franke & Piller, 2004; Piller et al., 2010; von Hippel, 1994; Witell et al., 2011). This is because sticky information is difficult to transfer as customers are not able to verbalize it. The easiest way to transfer sticky information is through close and direct customer-provider interactions (Ganesan, Malter, & Rindfleisch, 2005; Mahr, Lievens, & Blazevic, 2014): this is argued to be the major asset of co-creation (O'hern & Rindfleisch, 2010; Piller et al., 2010). Consequently, it is argued that the problem-solving perspective with its concept of sticky information is particularly appropriate for studying co-creation.

Taking a problem solving perspective on the co-creation of high-tech products, it is dealt with particularly ill-structured and fuzzy tasks because of the high level of uncertainty and information asymmetry due to non-existent or unclear problem definitions related to the high-tech domain (Alam, 2006; Olausson & Berggren, 2010). When business customers engage in joint problem solving activities with the provider (Lindgreen, Antioco, Palmer, & van Heesch, 2009), they often lack the necessary skills to articulate the desired knowledge elements by the provider (Nordin & Kowalkowski, 2010). In this context, Tuli et al. (2007) and Lapierre (1997) state that customers often do not have a precise understanding of their own needs that the provider seeks to gain (Bettencourt et al., 2002). This entails that the provider often struggles to elicit the sticky parts of information. This is also due to the significant information asymmetry in high-tech product co-creation that the provider must bridge for the co-creation success (Aarikka-Stenroos & Jaakkola, 2012; Nordin & Kowalkowski, 2010; Ulrich & Eppinger, 2012, p. 34; von Hippel, 1994).

Given these arguments, it is argued that co-creation is a specifically promising means to specify the high-tech product attributes from the problem-solving perspective, as it allows to face high levels of sticky information (Barley & Kunda, 2001; La Rocca et al., 2016; Nordin & Kowalkowski, 2010; Tuli et al., 2007) and to bridge the information asymmetry (Aarikka-Stenroos & Jaakkola, 2012; Alejandro et al., 2011; Ghosh et al., 2006). Finally, as von Hippel (1994) grounds his work within the specific context of technical, innovation-related problem solving, it is especially suitable as a theoretical lens for this dissertation with its high-tech focus.

2.4 Research gaps and needs

Overall, numerous studies call for further research that sheds light on the precise nature of co-creation processes for rather complex offerings such as high-tech (La Rocca et al., 2016; Madhavaram & Appan, 2010; Mustak et al., 2013; Olausson & Berggren, 2012). Salomonson et al. (2012) and Trischler, Pervan, and Scott (2017) stress the lack in extant literature to specifically focus on the interactive part, which is the co-creation process. Both studies found that many articles draw attention to the importance of the process, but neglect it in the empirical part. Also Madhavaram and Appan (2010) emphasize the importance for B2B companies to develop co-creation capabilities with emphasis on the process, yet research remains rather imprecise with according work (La Rocca et al., 2016; Olausson & Berggren, 2010). Further, Trischler et al. (2017) still denote co-creation processes as a *"black box"* in research (ibid., p. 265). As the success of the co-created product heavily relies on the process (Cui & Wu, 2017; Roberts et al., 2014), this is argued to be a serious omission in extant B2B research. Also, a recent work by Tidd and Bessant (2018) draws attention to the importance of innovating *processes*, as this promises greater returns than sheer product innovation. Considering this still under researched in innovation research (Biemans & Langerak, 2015; Mahr et al., 2014; Tidd & Bessant, 2018), there is a durable need to focus on co-creation *processes*. For the enhancement of the co-creation *process* in the context of high-tech products in the B2B domain, three research gaps are showcased in *Figure 3* and then outlined in the following:

1st research gap: Missing understanding how providers conduct the co-creation process Extant research falls short in understanding how providers involve, manage and engage business customers in the co-creation process for high-tech products.	**2nd research gap: Lacking comprehension of customer value of the co-creation process** The co-creation heavily relies on customer engagement. However, it must be understood what business customers value within the process.	**3rd research gap: Unexplored toolkit opportunities in the B2B high-tech domain** The usage of toolkits for facilitating co-creation processes is widely unexplored, while it promises high potentials to increase the efficiency of the overall process.

Figure 3: Three research gaps and needs in extant research

The *1st research gap* lies in the conduct of the co-creation process by the provider. As it has been shown, it is the provider's task to conduct the co-creation process (Aarikka-Stenroos & Jaakkola, 2012; Piller et al., 2010), but surprisingly few studies show how it needs to be carried out through the conducting company (Frow et al., 2015; Payne, Storbacka, & Frow, 2008). Characterized by joint problem solving between customer and provider, it is usually described as intense, because it starts off with a time-consuming understanding of what the provider must deliver to meet customers' needs (Davies, Brady, & Hobday, 2007; Tuli et al., 2007). One crucial challenge for rather complex offerings is that there is a significant information asymmetry between the parties involved, typically due to the specialization of the company (Teirlinck & Spithoven, 2013). The provider seeks to gain a thorough understanding of the customer's needs and practices; otherwise he struggles to deliver a solution that satisfies customers' needs (Payne et al., 2008). The better the knowledge delivered by the customer, the smoother is the joint product development (La Rocca et al., 2016), but extant research does not hold indications how to face this challenge. In conclusion, extant research lacks a clear picture of how providers involve, manage and engage customers in the co-creation processes of high-tech products in the B2B domain. This holds the opportunity to better comprehend how providers bridge information asymmetries and, from a problem-solving perspective, how they elicit the desired sticky information and solve the problem with the customer.

The *2nd research gap* refers to the customer value of the co-creation process of high-tech products. As mentioned, the co-creation success heavily relies on proper customer engagement. Therefore, it must be understood what customers value in co-creation processes (Hienerth & Lettl, 2011; Mustak et al., 2013; Roberts et al., 2014). Particularly, works by Biemans and Langerak (2015) and by Laage-Hellman et al. (2014) demand further research that focuses on the involvement of business customers, as ways to involve them *„tend to be different"* (ibid., p. 258) than the consumer domain. Moreover, in their bibliometric review on open innovation, Randhawa et al. (2016) call for an enhancement in co-creation research, delivering evidence that the collaboration with customers for new product development was a core topic in early open innovation research. But now, as they state, *"the focus on customers appears to have waned in more recent research"* (ibid., p. 768). In their conclusion, they demand a stronger focus on the customer in co-creation in innovation research. As a result, understanding the motivating factors to make customers engage in co-creation is necessary to strategically manage innovation processes (Biemans & Langerak, 2015; Frow et al., 2015; Hienerth & Lettl, 2011; Perks et al., 2012; Roberts et al., 2014). This topic is clearly set as one research priority in innovation research (Biemans & Langerak, 2015).

Coming to the *3rd research gap*, the literature on co-creating high-tech products has widely neglected opportunities of toolkits to support the co-creation process, while recent innovation studies call for tools that enable efficient co-creation (Barczak, 2012; Bstieler et al., 2018). As the efficiency and efficacy are major challenges in the co-creation of high-tech products (Gosling & Naim, 2009; La Rocca et al., 2016), toolkits with according purposes are promising. However, extant research has left it for the context of rather complex offerings, stating that potentials of toolkit support are very limited (Fauska et al., 2014; Salomonson et al., 2012). For instance, it is found that interactive processes between customer and provider are hard to transfer to an asynchronous solution, i. e. to a toolkit (Salomonson et al., 2012). Another study stresses that the suitability is limited because of the lack of rich media (Fauska et al., 2014; Laage-Hellman et al., 2014). In spite of this, according research appears especially useful due to the high potentials to facilitate the challenging processes as well as to lower costs (Laage-Hellman et al., 2014).

3 Context of the research

The empirical studies presented in this dissertation are carried out in the German high-tech textile industry within a collaborative, large-scale research initiative[10]. Two projects were conducted by the author within this initiative. Taking more than four years, the focus has been on co-creation as one pillar. Since this industry is characterized by high-tech products and a strong B2B focus, it is considered exemplary for the purposes of this dissertation. This *chapter* presents industry information with its brief history, peculiarities as well as product vignettes. More specific information, e. g. regarding the informants of the concrete companies participating at the studies in *Parts II, III* and *IV*, will be outlined in each study.

During the last decades, the textile industry in Germany has been exposed to heavy competition on the world market. Especially the Eastern part has been concerned, which has resulted in a massive reduction in employment from the 1990s (Beer, 2001; Fischer, 2003, p. 7). The clothing industry has been mainly impacted by that. This is why the industry has undergone a fundamental transformation process in the past decades: the textile industry has become more and more specialized in niches in the area of high-tech applications (Krippendorf, Holst, & Richter, 2009, p. 13). Thanks to that, the textile industry has reversed the downward trend of the 1990s significantly (Ebnet, 2014). It has grown especially in the area of customized technical textiles[11]. These high-tech textiles recorded substantial increases in turnover: between 1995 and 2006, it has grown by 30 % (Krippendorf et al., 2009, p. 13). At the same time, textile products such as house and home textiles have suffered massive losses, as these products typically constitute commodity products that are increasingly produced elsewhere (Adler, 2004;

[10] The research presented in this dissertation is strongly supported by the collaborative, large-scale research initiative *futureTEX* funded by the German Federal Ministry of Education and Research (BMBF). Within this context, two projects form the research context of this dissertation. The BMBF is greatly acknowledged for funding these projects within *futureTEX* (FKZ: 03ZZ0604A; 03ZZ0618B).

[11] Several recent empirical studies have been carried out within the German textile B2B industry, e. g. Gebhardt, Barteld, Grafmüller, Mosig, and Weiß (2017) focus on mass-customized technical textiles in the B2B domain; Rassmann and Grafmüller (2018) examine industry-specific drivers and barriers of sustainability; Mosig, Grafmüller, and Lehmann (2017) analyze business model patterns of German textile SMEs; and Grafmüller, Hankammer, Hönigsberg, and Wache (2018) set up a business process model that shows how a mass-customized high-tech textile is developed in a cross-organizational SME network.

Richter, 2007, p. 6). Mass production of cheap products has not been an appropriate strategy for these German companies anymore (Richter, 2007, p. 19). As a consequence, the focus has been put onto knowhow-intensive production. This has yielded innovative, high-tech products used mainly in industrial B2B contexts (Krippendorf et al., 2009, p. 34). Often, these high-tech products represent ETO products used in complex products and systems. The shift toward technical textiles is the main driver of the industry and it is assumed to accelerate during the next decades (Ebnet, 2014). Further, Germany is the market leader in this area of complex technical textiles, as a recent report shows (Gesamtverband textil+mode, 2017).

Table 3 gives insight into three product scenarios provided by this textile industry, including functions and also prospective stakeholder groups to be involved in co-creation. Afterwards, each scenario is showcased with a brief description.

Table 3: Examples on textile high-tech products with use cases

	Product with use case	**Exemplary functions/characteristics**	**Potential stakeholder groups involved**
I.	Smart textiles in the medical field	- Heating and glow - Sensory - Actuator properties	- Textile and electronical engineers - IT specialists - Experts from the final field of usage (e. g. doctors, medical staff) - Possibly other groups such as insurances etc.
II.	Technical textiles in architecture	- Translucence - Light-weight - Plasticity	- Textile engineers - Architects - Structural engineers - Different craftsmen
III.	Technical textiles in aerospace	- Cold, heat and sound insulation - Fire resistance - Light-weight	- Various textile engineers - Aircraft engineers - Safety experts (e. g. representatives from aircraft security)

Example I: Smart textiles in the medical field[12]

Figure 4: Example of a smart textile[13]

Smart textiles are equipped with functions such as heating, glow, or other sensory and actuator properties. As such textiles have to meet special requirements regarding wearability (Stoppa & Chiolerio, 2014), their development does not only bring together textile technology specialists with electronical engineers, but also experts from the intended field of usage. For instance doctors – hence the medical field, as health care exhibits an enormous potential for wearable technology (van Langenhove, 2007, pp. 4–7). Thereby, smart textiles offer great potential to be applied in clothes in order to improve, e. g., occupational safety (Dolez & Vu-Khanh, 2009). For that purposes, highly interdisciplinary development teams co-create such high-tech products as they require the expertise from different fields.

[12] Description and data are based on http://www.haute-innovation.com/de/magazin/smart-materials/smart-textiles-und-intelligente-oberflaechen.html, retrieved June 13 2018.

[13] Graphic is derived from http://www.titv-greiz.de/, retrieved June 13 2018.

Example II: Technical textiles in architecture[14]

Figure 5: Example of a technical textile in construction[15]

With coated fabrics as a form of technical textiles, new opportunities have emerged for construction and architecture. Even support-free constructions with wide spans and high translucence are possible, enabling novel design as *Figure 5* exhibits. Also for that purpose, stakeholders from various domains are needed for successful co-creating the high-tech products with its multi-faceted attributes, in this case including architects, structural engineers etc. besides the textile technology specialists.

[14] Description and data are drawn from https://www.sattler-global.com/textile-architecture/pvc-coated-polyester-fabrics-1075.jsp?lang=en, retrieved June 13 2018.

[15] Graphic is drawn from https://www.sattler-global.com/textile-architecture/pvc-coated-polyester-fabrics-1075.jsp?lang=en, retrieved June 13 2018.

Example III: Technical textiles in aerospace[16]

Figure 6: Example of a technical textile in aerospace[17]

With functions such as cold, heat, sound and fire insulation, technical textiles for aerospace are considered one exemplary high-tech application in the field of complex products and systems (Hobday & Rush, 1999). It is applied in aircrafts (see *Figure 6)* where it has to meet strict safety requirements and, regarding noise reduction, specific requirements by the customer for improvement cabin comfort. The development of such high-tech applications involves a series of different expertises.

The examples illustrate the required high interdisciplinarity of different fields to jointly develop the high-tech textile products. This makes the topic of co-creation particularly suitable and interesting in this domain. It is argued that this empirical field is particularly promising for the purposes of this dissertation for two reasons as follows. On the one hand, the great majority of the companies are SMEs (Adler, 2004; Gesamtverband textil+mode, 2017). SMEs are considered highly innovative as many of them are market

[16] Description and data are based on https://www.hutchinson.com/de/temperatur-und-schalld%C3%A4mmsysteme and https://standort-sachsen.de/sixcms/media.php/78/Branchenkatalog_LRI_Sachsen.pdf, both retrieved October 16 2018.

[17] Graphic is derived from https://www.hutchinson.com/de/temperatur-und-schalld%C3%A4mmsysteme, retrieved October 16 2018.

leaders in their specialized niches (Teirlinck, 2018; Teirlinck & Spithoven, 2013; Usman, Roijakkers, Vanhaverbeke, & Frattini, 2018), which holds true for the German textile sector with its clear emphasis on complex, technical textiles (Gesamtverband textil+mode, 2017, p. 4). Often, SMEs co-create products together with their customers to a higher degree than large enterprises (Spithoven, Vanhaverbeke, & Roijakkers, 2013). Moreover, SMEs are acknowledged for adopting new technologies early (Hochleitner, Arbussà, & Coenders, 2016). Last, mostly SMEs involve customers in co-creation processes as an open innovation tool (Usman et al., 2018; van de Vrande, Jong, Vanhaverbeke, & Rochemont, 2009). Therefore, the empirical field is heavily concerned with co-creating high-tech products – making it especially interesting for research.

4 Structure of the dissertation

The dissertation at hand encompasses five *parts* to better comprehend the co-creation of high-tech products in the B2B domain illustrated within the German textile industry. Each part contains one research step. The *parts* then follow the descending hierarchical structure of *chapters, sections* and *sub-sections*. *Part I* outlines the background of the co-creation of high-tech products, the theoretical framework, the research gaps in extant research, the domain of the context of this dissertation and eventually its structure. Moving on to the empirical part, the dissertation contains three empirical studies[18]. All of them individually explain the needs and objectives including background literature for each study. Their arrangement and interrelation is delineated in the following.

As both parties the provider and customer are naturally involved in co-creation processes, each party is dedicated one study in order to understand how companies can better manage co-creation in the high-tech B2B domain. With that goal, *Part II* addresses the first research gap. It commences with a study on unmasking promising practices to understand how providers master the task of co-creating high-tech products with their customers. Descriptions and results also help comprehend the underlying reasons why co-creation is such a challenging task in the B2B high-tech domain. In contrast, *Part III* focuses on the second research gap, namely the customer domain in co-creation: the goal is to analyze value components perceived by the customer throughout the process of co-creation. A better understanding of these value components is crucial to engage, motivate and appropriately involve customers in the co-creation of high-tech products. *Part II* and *Part III* are considered to be side by side, as their focus is either on the provider or the customer domain. Then, in *Part IV*, the emphasis is put on opportunities for IT support within the context of high-tech product co-creation, in line with the third research gap. The design-oriented study aims at building an artefact that is translated into a toolkit, which is tested in a real-life setting with both customer and provider. *Part V* encompasses a summary and an overarching discussion of the three

[18] The overall dissertation project with its three empirical studies was presented as an earlier version at the *R&D Management Conference PhD Colloquium* (*RADMA 2017*) in Leuven, Belgium, as well as at the Doctoral Colloquium of the *The 2017 World Mass Customization & Personalization Conference* (*MCPC 2017*), Aachen, Germany. All publications of the author are listed in *Annex I*.

empirical studies, followed by implications for research and managers. It concludes with the limitations and a final note by the author.

Figure 7 showcases an overview of the structure of the dissertation, followed by a brief description of the five parts. A detailed overview of the structure, content overview and outcomes is exhibited in *Figure 8*.

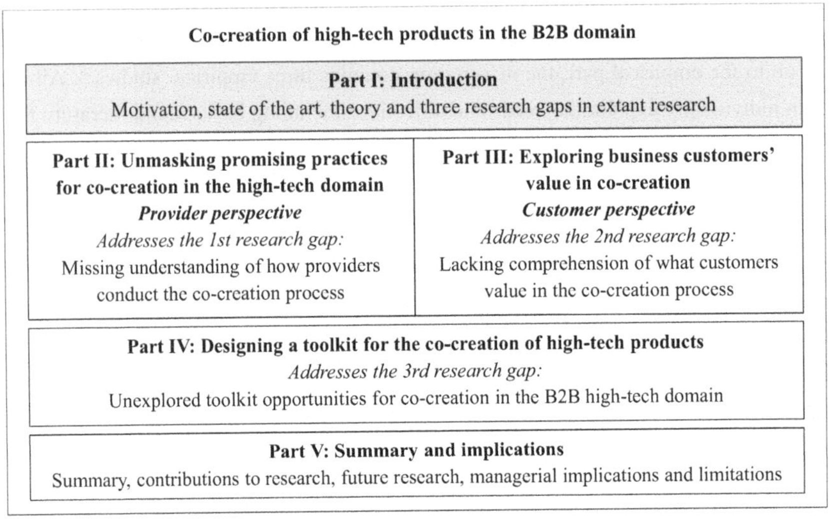

Figure 7: Structure of the dissertation

Part I: Introduction. Paving the way for the empirical studies, the *introduction* motivates the topic of co-creating high-tech products, exposes an overview of the theoretical framework and its state of the art in the literature. Based on that, it depicts three research gaps that are tackled by the empirical studies by the dissertation at hand. Further, insight into the German textile industry is given, which illustrates the context of the research at hand. *Part I* is concluded by the structure of the dissertation.

Part II – addressing the first research gap. Unmasking promising practices for co-creation in the high-tech domain. High-tech companies already embrace co-creation as a means to elicit customers' needs. The goal of this study is to understand how customers are managed and involved in co-creating high-tech products. With the ever-greater complexity, it seeks to unmask promising practices from a provider's perspective. The focus is on practices that have developed informally. An explorative study is undertaken to unmask according practices. In the German textile high-tech industry, 29 interviews were conducted with managers that are primarily involved in co-creation. The findings exhibit four promising practices explained in detail. For instance, it is outlined how incorrect specifications are avoided by insisting on visiting both the provider's site and the customer's site. Another practice provides a precise understanding of how physical spaces are created, for instance by means of organizing an 'Innovation Day' with diverse stakeholders. This study primarily delivers a better understanding of how high-tech products are co-created nowadays, and how customers are involved in these challenging processes by the provider.

Part III – addressing the second research gap. Exploring business customers' value in co-creation. Co-creation is acknowledged as a powerful means to elicit customer needs in high-tech product development. But despite the numerous studies in the field, it remains unclear what business customers actually value in co-creation processes. More precisely, a series of studies draws a clear picture of functional value components, but more recent studies also indicate the importance of emotional and social value in B2B co-creation. To explore the phenomenon of emotional and social value, 42 business customers were interviewed. All of them are industrial buyers in the high-tech textile industry in Germany, all having an engineering background. The results unveil three novel value components for the B2B domain. For instance, in contrast to the acknowledged picture of the rational business customer, data stress the importance of the emotional value component *playfulness*. Being novel to B2B research, it is argued for major consequences in manifold regards.

Part IV – addressing the third research gap. Designing a toolkit for the co-creation of high-tech products. Opportunities of toolkit support in the co-creation of high-tech products are widely neglected. On the one hand, this appears obvious because high-tech products are best co-created in face-to-face settings. On the other hand, this assumption is likely to fall short in considering how to capture lower levels of sticky information. Lower levels of sticky information are typically also part of the required information. Moreover, this is helpful for the provider to better prepare the face-to-face interaction, which allows reducing information costs. With that goal, a toolkit is designed in cooperation with B2B companies of the German high-tech textile industry. Following design-oriented research, an artefact is developed, based on data from five focus groups. The artefact is a use case diagram highlighting four identified functions. E. g., the function *specifying the final use of the product* is crucial with its implications for the overall process. Then, for one of the companies, an artefact-based toolkit is built along the company's specific product portfolio specifications and its decision tree. The iterative evaluation process is informed by seven in-depth interviews, and it is described how the toolkit captures required information in the co-creation of high-tech products.

Part V: Discussion: Co-creating high-tech products. Part V encompasses a summary and an overarching discussion of the three empirical studies, also discussing the rigor of this research. Afterwards, managerial implications and future avenues of research are exposed. Special emphasis is put on industry peculiarities with regard to limitations for related industries.

Co-creation of high-tech products in the B2B domain

I. Introduction

- Motivation of the topic
- Framing, state of the art in the literature and theory
- Three research gaps in extant research
- Context of the research
- Structure of this dissertation

II: Unmasking promising practices for co-creation in the high-tech domain

- Explores promising practices from the provider's perspective
- Uses a QDA with 1st order themes and 2nd order concepts for its 29 interviews
- Unmasks four promising practices
- Provides a better understanding of how customers are managed, engaged and involved in co-creating high-tech products

III. Exploring business customer's value in co-creation

- Explores the neglected areas of emotional and social value in B2B from the customer's perspective
- Uses a thematic content analysis for its 42 interviews
- Unveils three value components novel to B2B research
- Delivers rich insight into the customer's perceived value of the co-creation process

IV. Designing a toolkit for the co-creation of high-tech products

- Explores the opportunities of toolkit support in co-creation
- Aims to collect information with the toolkit that allows the provider for better preparing the face-to-face interaction
- Follows design-oriented research with artefact development, toolkit demonstration and evaluation in a real-life setting
- Uses five focus groups and seven in-depth interviews, all examined using a QDA
- The artefact is a use case diagram highlighting four identified functions, that are translated in an actionable toolkit
- Findings help describe how the toolkit is usable for co-creation of high-tech products

V. Summary and implications

- Summary
- Contribution to research
- Avenues for further research
- Managerial implications
- Concluding remarks with limitations and final notes

Figure 8: Outline of the dissertation

Part II – Unmasking promising practices for co-creation in the high-tech domain

L. K. Grafmüller, *Co-Creation of High-Tech Products in the B2B Domain*,
Markt- und Unternehmensentwicklung Markets and Organisations,
https://doi.org/10.1007/978-3-658-28412-1_2

1 Needs and objectives[19]

> *"More research is needed to examine the various aspects of customer participation in the creation of business-to-business offerings, including [...] sellers' potential to facilitate [the] participation [of business customers]."* (Mustak et al., 2013, p. 352)

Part I introduced the relevance, state of the art in extant literature and also set the context of the research for this dissertation. It becomes evident that there is a need to better understand co-creation processes in the B2B domain. With that aim, this *part* picks up the first research gap (see *Chapter 2* of *Part I*) and unveils promising practices of how providers manage and involve business customers into the co-creation of high-tech products. It is embedded in the dissertation as illustrated in *Figure 9*:

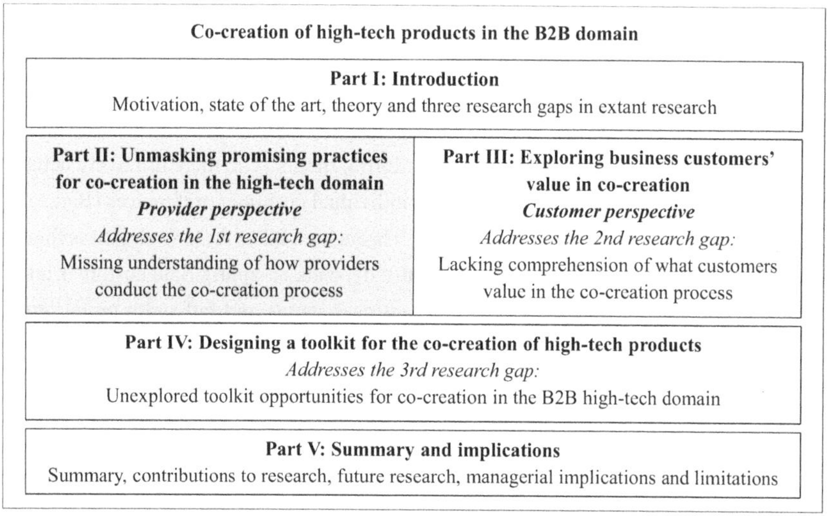

Figure 9: Embedding of *Part II* in the dissertation

[19] An earlier version of this study has been presented at the *2017 R&D Management Conference*, Leuven, Belgium, as well as at the *XXVIII ISPIM Innovation Conference*, Vienna, Austria. All publications of this dissertation's author are listed in *Annex I*. An updated version of this research is prepared for journal publication with the authors Grafmüller, Velamuri, & Möslein.

A more detailed need for this study with the derivation of the research question (RQ) to address the first research gap (see *Figure 9*) is outlined in the following.

Recent research has noticed a rising number of B2B companies that involve customers in innovation and co-creation (Kohtamäki & Rajala, 2016; La Rocca et al., 2016; Malshe & Friend, 2018). This is particularly pronounced in high-tech domains, where high product complexity is a challenging task to master in joint development projects. Here, customers are heavily involved in innovation activities (La Rocca et al., 2016; Madhavaram & Appan, 2010; Olausson & Berggren, 2012). Moreover, the degree of customer involvement is constantly increasing (Laage-Hellman et al., 2014). Extant research emphasizes one major reason, often taking a problem-solving perspective (Aarikka-Stenroos & Jaakkola, 2012; von Hippel, 1994): co-creation is promising to elicit customer requirements they cannot verbalize, namely sticky information (Nordin & Kowalkowski, 2010; Tuli et al., 2007; von Hippel, 1994).

Sticky information is especially crucial in high-tech product development (La Rocca et al., 2016), because the level of such information is very high in this context (Nordin & Kowalkowski, 2010; von Hippel, 1994). This highlights the importance of managing the co-creation process (Harmancioglu et al., 2007). In this vein, there is a lively debate on designing co-creation processes along the individual customer preferences (Barczak, 2012; Frow et al., 2015; Roberts et al., 2014). Throughout all of these studies, it is found that the overall success of co-creation crucially depends on appropriate customer integration. Or, in other words, the co-creation success stands and falls with proper customer engagement (La Rocca et al., 2016; Roberts et al., 2014; Vaquero Martín et al., 2016). For this end, it is the provider's task to lead, manage and structure the co-creation process (Aarikka-Stenroos & Jaakkola, 2012; Piller et al., 2010). However, research lacks an understanding of current practices of the co-creation process of high-tech products.

This study follows the assumption that B2B firms must have developed practices to face the present product complexity in co-creation processes. Especially, *promising practices* are at the center of interest (Bessant, Kaplinsky, & Lamming, 2003; Leseure, Bauer, Birdi, Neely, & Denyer, 2004). Such practices enable firms to successfully manage co-creation processes and serve to understand how companies conduct co-creation in the B2B high-tech domain. Accordingly, *Part II* targets the first research gap of this dissertation by unmasking promising practices. Such practices are used by the provider and do not represent a formal guideline, but are rather practices that have progressively developed over time. Based on that, the RQ for this empirical part reads:

> *RQ to address the first research gap:*
> *What practices enable firms to successfully manage and involve customers in the co-creation of high-tech products?*

A better understanding of current practices of co-creating high-tech products promises enhancements for customer engagement as well as the design of according co-creation processes (Barczak, 2012; Biemans & Langerak, 2015; Frow et al., 2015; Madhavaram & Appan, 2010). Furthermore, it sheds light on its peculiarities and underlying challenges. These points help increase efficacy and efficiency of the co-creation process, both hotspots in high-tech product development (Davies et al., 2007; Gosling & Naim, 2009; Madhavaram & Appan, 2010; Olausson & Berggren, 2012). For instance, it supports the correct product specification with the customer, which innovation research often emphasizes as crucial (Hobday, 1998; Hobday & Rush, 1999). Overall, a better understanding of co-creation allows for exploiting the large potentials that lie in effective innovation processes (Madhavaram & Appan, 2010; Stockstrom & Herstatt, 2008; Vaquero Martín et al., 2016).

Taking a problem-solving perspective, an explorative study was undertaken in the German high-tech textile industry to unmask promising practices. 29 managers were interviewed during on-site company visits, who are all mainly concerned with the co-creation of high-tech textile products. Challenges in this branch are, for instance, great uncertainties regarding the final use of the high-tech product. Moreover, co-creation processes also touch upon the demonstration of intangible functions such as fire resistance, heat insulation, and noise damping, which are particularly hard to explain. A qualitative data analysis following Gioia, Corley, and Hamilton (2013) is conducted to unmask 1st order concepts, 2nd order themes as well as aggregate dimensions for this study's purposes. In total, four promising practices are exhibited and described in-depth.

Part II of the dissertation contains five *chapters. Chapter 1* presented the embedding of the study with its needs and objectives. Then, *Chapter 2* sets out the theoretical underpinning. *Chapter 3* focuses on the research design by detailing the sampling, data collection, and data analysis. *Chapter 4* showcases the findings with underlying challenges. Finally, *Chapter 5* concludes *Part II* with a contribution to research, managerial implications and avenues for further research.

2 Theoretical underpinning

Chapter 2 sets out the relevant theoretical underpinnings for this empirical study. From a provider's view, the first *section* focuses on underlying challenges to co-create high-tech products, the second *section* deals with the problem-solving perspective on the topic and, finally, the third *section* is dedicated to practices-related research of high-tech product co-creation in the B2B domain.

2.1 Underlying challenges: Co-creating high-tech products

The co-creation process is facilitated by the company (Aarikka-Stenroos & Jaakkola, 2012; Piller et al., 2011). Consequently, it is a management task to ensure effective and efficient processes (Harmancioglu et al., 2007). However, while the effects of involving B2B customers in innovation (Alam, 2006) and proper management of early innovation phases (Verworn, Herstatt, & Nagahira, 2008) have been found positive, there is a shortcoming in extant research how to face the challenges involved (Frow et al., 2015; La Rocca et al., 2016; Malshe & Friend, 2018; Mustak et al., 2013). To better comprehend this from a provider's viewpoint, it makes sense to set out the three main challenges when providers conduct co-creation processes for high-tech products, as illustrated in *Figure 10*. The following paragraphs depict these challenges to lay the basis for this empirical study.

Time intensity: Intense face-to-face interactions often entail a lack of efficiency.	**Requirement capturing:** High product complexity increases the likelihood of incorrect specifications.	**Customer engagement:** If customers are not properly engaged, the co-creation success is jeopardized.

Figure 10: Challenges to co-create high-tech products from a provider's view

The *time intensity* of co-creating high-tech products is a result of several reasons. Most notably, there is a strong need to explain the intricate attributes, which takes place in an intense customer-provider interaction (Fauska et al., 2014). Typically, this is done via personal interactions, because high-tech products are best explained in face-to-face settings (Heide & John, 1990; La Rocca et al., 2016; Vaquero Martín et al., 2016). Samples and prototypes are typically used to explain intricate attributes of the offering (Ghosh et al., 2006), or more abstract boundary objects (Star, 1989). As face-to-face is considered rather time-consuming, this interaction runs into danger of lacking efficiency (Davies et al., 2007; Gosling & Naim, 2009).

The *requirement capturing* from the customer is crucial to co-create a product that matches customer's needs. Extant research highlights the role of the provider to elicit customer's requirements in high-tech product development properly (Aarikka-Stenroos & Jaakkola, 2012). Because in the event of incorrect specifications, there are major cost overruns, customer (and provider) dissatisfaction as well as project delays (Hobday, 1998; Nightingale, 2000). As a consequence, there is a lack of both efficiency and efficacy of the co-creation process (Davies et al., 2007; Gosling & Naim, 2009).

The topic of *customer engagement* becomes more and more important with the increasing degree of customer involvement in co-creation (Laage-Hellman et al., 2014; Malshe & Friend, 2018). It is so important, because the overall innovation success of the co-creation relies on appropriate customer engagement (Hienerth & Lettl, 2011; La Rocca et al., 2016; Roberts et al., 2014; Vaquero Martín et al., 2016). Although found to be a major process driver (Mustak et al., 2013; Roberts et al., 2014), rather little is known on how providers actively engage the business customer in the co-creation process. E. g., a recent study by Malshe and Friend (2018) delivers empirical evidence: the authors expose 'non-receptive' business customers, hence customers who are unwilling to engage in co-creation. As a result, there is still an ongoing need to understand how to involve and motivate business customers in the co-creation of high-tech products (Madhavaram & Appan, 2010; Mustak et al., 2013; Vaquero Martín et al., 2016).

2.2 A provider's view on sticky information and promising practices

According to the problem-solving perspective, the provider is in charge of acquiring the information by the customer that the company seeks (Nickerson & Zenger, 2004), namely the sticky information (von Hippel, 1994). To achieve that, the provider must face the challenges described in *Figure 10* to elicit the desired information (Simon, 1978). In this context, Simon (1973) argues that a problem solver, which is the provider in this case, informally develops routines to solve ill-structured tasks. Hence, the provider seeks to solve a complex problem, which is the elicitation of sticky information by means of the co-creation process in the present context, by developing routines to face that challenge. More precisely, Simon (1973) elaborates on that by suggesting that a problem solver develops *"possible programs (strategies)"* (ibid., p. 273) to face complexity. These routines that evolve from joint problem solving are at the center of interest in this study, but they are conceptualized as *promising practices,* for several reasons.

Practices are termed promising when they are considered to lead to better performance (Leseure et al., 2004). The research on promising practices is about archetypes of management practices that have been gradually developed and tested, forming *"a coherent, integrated whole, which can be described as commonly repeatable configuration of distinct elements"* (Leseure et al., 2004, p. 170). They are not *best practices*, because they are rather dynamic, requiring constant improvement, and they are not only *routines,* as Simon (1973) calls them, because they clearly aim for improving the performance. Promising practices need to be customized from time to time, taking the dynamic into consideration (Bessant et al., 2003).

Given these arguments, promising practices are considered particularly suitable through the problem-solving lens to study how providers elicit sticky information. This is also called for in a number of studies with a special emphasis on actual practices of joint development processes (Backman et al., 2007; Frow et al., 2015; Kohtamäki & Rajala, 2016; Vaquero Martín et al., 2016). Further, promising practices are powerful to deeply describe approaches of co-creation that *"lead to valuable discoveries"* (Kohtamäki & Rajala, 2016, p. 11). Also, a clearer picture of current practices of established processes, grown modes of interaction or typical procedures allows for understanding how providers elicit sticky information (Ganesan et al., 2005; Mahr et al., 2014; Piller et al., 2010; von Hippel, 1994), for enhancing the customer engagement as well as the design of according co-creation processes (Barczak, 2012; Frow et al., 2015; Madhavaram & Appan, 2010).

2.3 Practices-related research on co-creating high-tech products

Looking at the literature what practices providers use to design the co-creation process in order to elicit the customer's information, extant research does not shed light on actual practices, but holds rather indications (Frow et al., 2015). *Table 4* provides an overview of relevant studies that deal with B2B co-creation of rather complex offerings.

Table 4: Practices-related studies on the co-creation of rather complex offerings

Author	Finding	Method used
Laage-Hellman et al. (2014)	Providers should promote openness to involve customers properly in joint product development processes.	Qualitative case study, mainly interviews
Vaquero Martín et al. (2016)	Business customers are unlikely to value enjoyment in the process. Capabilities for stakeholder integration are, e. g., involving both right and diverse stakeholders, appropriate interaction, using boundary objects.	Conceptual research & systematic literature review
Haas et al. (2012)	Relevant tasks to designing the NPD process are two-way communication, enabling mutual learning constantly and activating relevant actors.	Conceptual research & interviews
Hakanen and Jaakkola (2012)	Defining the core content of a co-created solution is a major challenge, also because customers do not want to share sufficient information. Also, different customer types are described regarding the involvement they wish.	Qualitative, multiple case studies, mainly interviews
Aarikka-Stenroos and Jaakkola (2012)	One crucial task for the provider is to help the customer articulate his needs, enabling him to make right decisions by intense explaining. Provider key activity is to be the process organizer.	Qualitative, mainly interviews
Jaakkola and Hakanen (2013)	The customer-provider interaction is prerequisite for designing, developing, and implementing the high-tech product. However, several customers want minimal involvement.	Qualitative, multiple case studies, mainly interviews
Hohenschwert and Geiger (2015)	Main task of provider of complex offerings is to explain intricate characteristics, typically supported by boundary objects.	Shadowing technique observations
Prior (2013)	Customers wish efficiency, anxiety reduction in the process, trust in ability and proper process conduct.	Exploratory netnography
Madhavaram and Appan (2010)	Co-creation capability is one operant resource for developing complex B2B products. Companies need to expand it to make the process of developing high-tech products more efficient and/or effective.	Conceptual research
Malshe and Friend (2018)	Some business customers are 'non-receptive' and unwilling to co-create from time to time, which requires particular approaches to involve them in co-creation.	Qualitative, interviews

When stating that the studies contain rather indications, this means that the literature often falls short in being explicit on how to involve business customers. For instance, in their case study on B2B customer involvement conducted at a large truck provider, Laage-Hellman et al. (2014) focus on *"'how' [...] Volvo uses customers in product development"*[20] (ibid., p. 269). One key finding is that providers should promote openness: *"[...] the Volvo case illustrates [...] that managers should be more open"* (ibid., p. 273). However, despite their goal to focus on how a company actually conducts joint development, their findings do not explain how the provider achieves, as in the given example, more openness. The other studies provided in *Table 4* are analogously implicit looking at how to involve customers in the co-creation of high-tech products. As a result, based on these studies, it is argued that there is a strong need for better understanding how providers actually conduct co-creation processes of high-tech products, especially to elicit sticky information.

This argument is in line with several calls for further research on the management of complexity in customer-provider interactions (Aarikka-Stenroos & Jaakkola, 2012; Madhavaram & Appan, 2010; Prior, 2013) with business customers (Malshe & Friend, 2018; Mustak et al., 2013). As a consequence, it is argued for the need to draw a clearer picture of how providers engage business customers in high-tech product co-creation. This also expands the understanding of underlying lines of thought in this domain to benefit from its explanatory and descriptive power (Tidd & Bessant, 2018).

In order to draw this clearer picture, this study aims at unveiling practices used by the provider to conduct co-creation processes for high-tech products in the B2B domain. As high-tech products seem to be co-created nowadays already, it is expected that practices have gradually developed over time. This is why this study aims to understand how the abovementioned challenges are faced by unmasking *promising practices* in this context.

[20] Emphasis of 'how' adopted by the authors Laage-Hellman et al. (2014).

3 Method and data

Chapter 3 depicts the method and data of the first empirical study presented in *Part II*. The first *section* advocates for a qualitative research approach that is afterwards detailed in the second *section* with the research design, including the sampling, data collection and well as data analysis.

3.1 Research approach

This study seeks to answer the question what practices enable firms to successfully manage and involve customers in the co-creation of high-tech products. The overall context is described in *Part I* and deeper explained in the latter *sections* of *Part II*. Since extant research has not looked at promising practices how customers are integrated in the co-creation of high-tech products, a qualitative approach appears suitable to unmask and deeper explain current practices with its underlying challenges.

Considered adequate for better conceptual development and understanding of phenomena (Eisenhardt, 1989), the qualitative research approach allows for comprehending and asking the study participants *why* and *how* they developed the promising practices in the context of high-tech product co-creation. Looking at the promising practices aimed at, one goal is to unveil the underlying lines of thought or gradual developments of the practices that providers evolved. More precisely, the emphasis is on practices that have informally developed over time as it is assumed that complexity in co-creation is faced already. This is why the study follows the structure by Gioia et al. (2013) which is acknowledged for an adequate data presentation showing also underlying lines of argument. Exploratory in nature, this research approach is powerful to explain and elicit in-depth information within the given context (Yin, 2014, p. 5). With that aim, every actor within these SMEs who is in touch with co-creation was involved in this interview study.

3.2 Sample and data

This study was conducted within the high-tech textile industry in Germany[21]. This branch provides textiles for specific applications such as heat and acoustic insulation. Since intangible characteristics are part of the highly technical products, this is considered a difficult task in co-creation. The companies participating in this study provide high-tech textiles for furniture, coated fabrics and technical textiles (see *Annex II* for a detailed overview) and have the following three commonalities. First, their core business is providing high-tech products. They are ETO companies which typically develop a part of the offering for each customer exclusively. Thereby, companies are in touch with customer involvement in their daily business. Second, within the process, there is typically a high degree of offline interaction. So salespeople are required to minimize complexity and reduce uncertainty. Third, companies are SMEs in B2B markets and specialized in very specific domains. Their business model embraces serving niche markets to satisfy the demand for specific high-tech applications. As SMEs are generally acknowledged for high technological innovativeness and open innovation enablers (Hochleitner et al., 2016; Teirlinck & Spithoven, 2013; Usman et al., 2018), this appears suitable for the goal of this study.

Since the companies lead the co-creation process (Aarikka-Stenroos & Jaakkola, 2012; Piller et al., 2011), the sampling criterion for the selection of the interviewees was to include the major actors involved in co-creation. Following the purposeful sampling approach (Patton, 1990), CEOs, salespeople, technical directors, and development managers were inquired, because these groups are at the center of co-creating high-tech products with the customer (Haas et al., 2012). In the SMEs, often the CEO himself is heavily concerned with co-creation, which is why a series of interviews is conducted on this level. To ensure rich and valuable insights, only actors with an experience of more than ten years in this area were included. The different branches and the interview database are shown in *Table 5*.

[21] A description of the context of this research with examples is provided in *Part I, Chapter 3*.

Table 5: Overview of sample and interview database of *Part II*

Industry sector	Firm	Brief description	Names (anonymized)	Interview length	Location	Position of interviewee	Staff
Furniture Fabrics	Furn_1	High-quality fabric manufacturer with specific functions for outdoor use, e. g., waterproof, tear-proof	Christian, Tom	2h 7min	Hof	CEO, Sales Manager	75
	Furni_2	High-quality fabric manufacturer with specific functions for indoor use, e. g., acoustic insulating and fireproof	Jörg, Martin	2h 18min	Chemnitz	Sales Manager, Technical Director	50
	Furn_3	High-quality fabric manufacturer with specific functions for indoor use, e. g., acoustic & heat insulating, fireproof	Björn, Kerstin	1h 51min	Chemnitz	Sales Manager, Development Manager	75
	Furn_4	High-quality fabric manufacturer with specific functions for indoor use, e. g., acoustic & heat insulating, fireproof	Gabriel	57min	Chemnitz	CEO	25
	Furn_5	High-quality fabric manufacturer with specific functions for indoor use, e. g., acoustic & heat insulating, fireproof	Leif, Bernd	2h 3min	Dresden	CEO, Sales Manager	25
Coated Fabrics	Coated_1	Manufacturer of coated fabrics with specific functions, e. g., tear-proof, heat-resistant, cold-resistant, embossment	Katja, Jonas	2h 9min	Zwickau	CEO, Technical Director	150
	Coated_2	Manufacturer of coated fabrics with specific functions, e. g., heat-resistant, cold-resistant, resilience	Marcus, Melanie	2h 11min	Dresden	CEO, Sales Manager	50
	Coated_3	Manufacturer of coated fabrics with specific functions, e. g., heat-resistant, cold-resistant, resilience	Carl	54min	Chemnitz	CEO	25
	Coated_4	Service provider for coated fabrics, adding specific functions, e. g., soft hand, impregnation	Inge	1h 2min	Zwickau	Sales Manager	25
	Coated_5	Service provider for coated fabrics, adding specific functions, e. g., soft hand, biocidal treatment	Maria, Markus	2h 7min	Chemnitz	CEO, Development Manager	50
Technical Textiles	Tech_1	Manufacturer of yarn for technical textiles with specific functions, e. g., tensile strength, heat- & cold-resistant	Petra, Greg	2h 21min	Chemnitz	CEO, Sales Manager	100
	Tech_2	Manufacturer of lightweight non-wovens with specific functions, e. g., acoustic & heat insulating	Horst, Bernd	2h 2min	Zwickau	Technical Director, Sales Manager	200
	Tech_3	Manufacturer of non-wovens with specific functions, e. g., acoustic & heat insulating	Dietmar	55min	Dresden	CEO	25
	Tech_4	Service provider for technical textiles, adding specific functions, e. g., biocidal treatment, impregnation	Gregor, Hugo	2h 4min	Chemnitz	Sales Managers	100
	Tech_5	Service provider for technical textiles, adding specific functions, e. g., water-resistant, fireproof	Andreas, Bert	2h 22min	Zwickau	CEO, Technical Director	100
	Tech_6	Service provider for technical textiles, adding specific functions, e. g., water-resistant, fireproof	Anno, Friedrich, Anja	3h 14min	Chemnitz	CEO, Technical Director, Sales Manager	125
In total			**29 interviews**	**30h 47min**			

Data for this study was gathered by the author of this dissertation in personal meetings, always combined with a company inspection including the production site and the different departments. While the main data for this study are tape-recorded interviews, the database also comprises desk research about the company conducted by the research before the company visits, and field notes taken during the interviews and the company inspection. In total, 29 interviews were conducted during 16 visits in different companies. Visits took around five hours, and approximately 120 minutes were dedicated exclusively to the purposes of this study. The interviews took 64 minutes on average; the shortest was 49 minutes. The interview database encompasses 30 hours 47 minutes in total, all audiotaped and transcribed. Following Fusch and Ness (2015), the database is considered both thick and rich because it comprises a large database, and because it is detailed and nuanced. Data gathering was stopped when data saturation was sufficient and when intricate phenomena were deeply explained by various interviewees (Fusch & Ness, 2015).

As multiple informal practices were assumed, a semi-structured interview approach was chosen. Following Yin (2014, p. 69), the interview guideline was flexibly adapted throughout data collection. Interviews followed a guideline based on topics drawn from the literature (see *Table 6*). Encompassing three blocks regarding the organization of the co-creation process, customer involvement and prevention of incorrect specifications, it was sought to uncover as many process details as possible to deeply explain and unveil promising practices. It was asked, for instance, *how and what customers are involved in co-creation? What are good and bad practices from your experience?* Interviewees were asked to elaborate freely on the open questions. Then, to move into the details, further inquiries especially aimed to elicit in-depth information on underlying trains of thought, asking *why* follow-up questions such as *why do you meet the customer in person in the early phase?* The interview guideline, shown in *Table 6,* was improved throughout the process (Miles, Huberman, & Saldaña, 2014). More precisely, it was based on the constant comparative method by Glaser (1965), following a three-step approach illustrated in *Figure 11.* Further, these three steps are also in line with Tracy (2010) in order to improve the quality of the qualitative research by mirroring preliminary results with co-creation managers at mid-term.

Table 6: Interview guideline for *Part II*

Focal area	Questions
1. Organizing and conducting the co-creation process	Please describe a *typical* co-creation process (regarding time, place, mode of interaction etc.) (e. g. Aarikka-Stenroos & Jaakkola, 2012; Fang et al., 2008).
	From your experience, what are good and bad practices (if possible, elaborate on anecdotes and/or on gradual practice improvements)?
	How do you conduct the overall process? What parts of the process do you structure, and what parts remain unstructured? (Olausson & Berggren, 2010)
2. Involving the business customer	How are customers integrated (Piller et al., 2011) and what customers (Haas et al., 2012) are involved in co-creation?
	How do you elicit the customer knowledge that you require? (e. g. Nordin & Kowalkowski, 2010)
	How do you motivate the customer to engage in the process? (e. g. Füller, Faullant, & Matzler, 2010)
	How deep do you involve the customer? And how long throughout the process? (for breadth and depth, see e. g. Fang et al., 2008)
	Regarding different customer preferences (Hakanen & Jaakkola, 2012), how do you adapt the process accordingly?
3. Facing high product complexity	What means do you use to face high product complexity (i. e. routines, practices, strategies)? How are customers enabled to deal with high product complexity? (e. g. Olausson & Berggren, 2012)
	How do you avoid incorrect and late-discovered specifications? (e. g. Cooper, 1999)
	What practices have you developed to systematically capture customer requirements? (Bare & Cox, 2008)
Depending on the responses, *how* and *why* questions followed to better understand underlying trains of thought and to understand *why* certain practices have developed in the form they are used by the provider (see e. g. Teirlinck, 2018). This especially served to understand original challenges and the gradual development of the promising practices.	

In a last step, all interviewees were invited to a workshop organized by the author of this research. To that occasion, results were discussed and evaluated at a one-day workshop with 14 out of 29 surveyed providers.

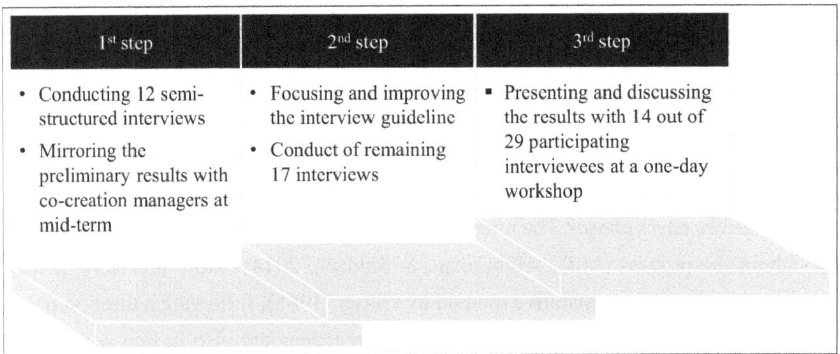

Figure 11: Three-step approach of data collection

3.3 Data analysis

The qualitative data analysis was based on the coding procedure suggested by Corbin and Strauss (2008) and the structure by Gioia et al. (2013). Starting with initial codes based on first topics related to practices, the code list was revised and expanded in an iterative process and constantly compared (Glaser, 1965; Miles et al., 2014). The goal of this method is both to reflect constructs drawn from the literature and to explore new constructs based on the data. This approach combines deductive and inductive elements of qualitative research (Glaser, 1965). In the following, the process of data analysis of this study is described more precisely.

At first, the database was scanned while looking through the problem-solving lens for actual practices used by the provider in the co-creation process. Activities were marked and interpretations for categories as *promising practices* were developed. Bearing on the data representation by Gioia et al. (2013), the 1st order concepts represent actual statements by the interviewees and 2nd order themes exhibit interpretations and the categorization. More precisely, this shows the process of data analysis, as the 2nd order themes represent one interpretation step that is based on the 1st order concept. Subsequently, another coding cycle followed for identifying the essence of the data and enriching the patterns within the database. Then, four aggregate dimensions were developed and grounded in the data in the last coding cycle (Gioia et al., 2013).

Two examples of how the coding procedure led to discovering an aggregate dimension are delineated in the following. It illustrates how either implicit or explicit statements by the interviewees have been interpreted. Looking through the problem-solving lens for practices of co-creating high-tech products, the researcher encounters the following statement by a technical director:

> *"We disclose every single parameter and play with an open hand. There's no easier way to build trust than to share some secret information."*

This quote includes an actual activity for co-creation (*playing with an open hand*) and thereby represents an explicit statement. In the first step, the researcher coded this segment both 'opening up' and 'building trust'. The according 1st order concept was labeled 'demonstrate own openness by sharing knowledge' (see *Figure 13* for the Gioia structure) which semantically appeared useful as it includes both an activity as well as its underlying goal. The 2nd order theme, representing the superordinate category, was entitled 'opening up oneself'. This concept and theme was then iteratively improved, revised and aligned, specifically on a terminological level. Later, the iterative coding procedure led the researcher to inductively developing the aggregate dimension of the underlying concept and theme, namely 'building an open and trustful relationship'.

Another interview excerpt exhibits a theme implicitly:

> *"We are probably the only ones in Europe who can really handle that technology. So we can open up everything, why not? Others can't copy our know-how anyway."*

Here, although the coder did not consider the statement *"can open up everything"* an actual activity, he found the theme of opening up. This segment was assigned to the theme 'opening up oneself' in the second step, when the researcher was mainly concerned with searching patterns within the formerly aligned code list. This step particularly aimed at a better understanding of the phenomena under study, and this segment was considered useful to explain underlying motives in the high-tech domain.

The coder used the QDA software ATLAS.ti that provides *Figure 12* with the illustration of the four promising practices (dark grey) with 2nd order themes. The presentation of findings with discussion, also issuing the 1st order concepts, follows in the subsequent section.

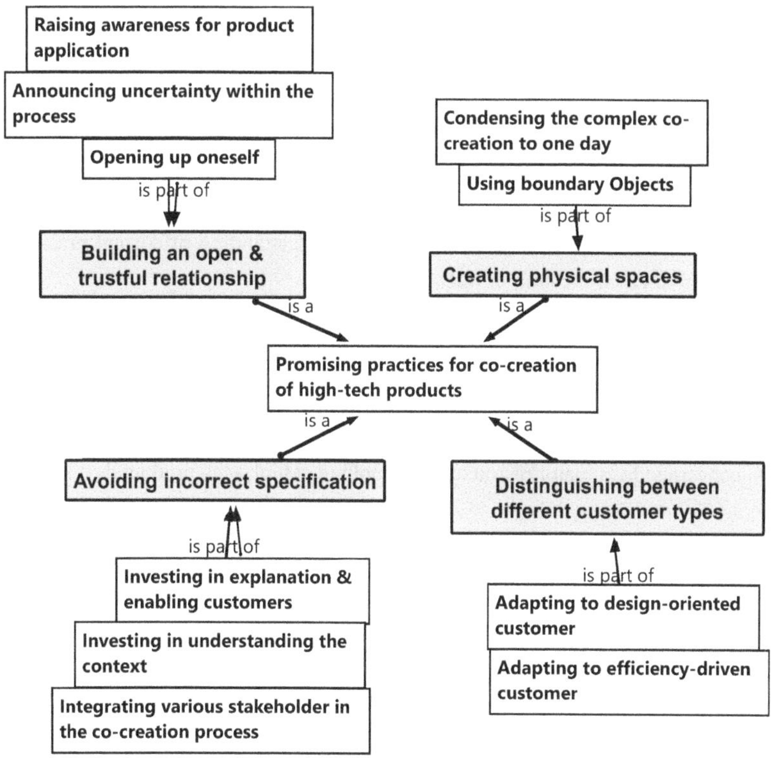

Figure 12: Code overview for promising practices for high-tech product co-creation

To improve the quality of interview data interpretations, additional data sources were used (Tracy, 2010): findings of the interview analysis were both combined with field notes and presented at a workshop that took place with the interviewees.

4 Findings

Chapter 4 presents the findings from the qualitative data analysis and exhibits the promising practices for co-creating high-tech products in the B2B domain. Specifically, the emphasis is put on a detailed presentation of the database in order to illuminate the promising practices to face the challenges of high product complexity in co-creation. Overall, it is argued that this provides a better understanding of current practices of high-tech product co-creation in B2B.

To commence, the subsequent quote overarches the data as well as the credo of the 29 interviews conducted with CEOs, salespeople, technical directors as well as development managers. As an opening quote, this underpins that the interviewees have been concerned by a major restructuration looking at high-tech product development:

> *Andreas: "Fifteen years ago, the market was completely non-transparent. Customers couldn't look into companies at all. They didn't have a clue how we work. That has become impossible with today's complexity. Everybody noticed that it's just not possible for the know-how to be handled by just one person: we totally opened up our processes."*

As the code overview in *Figure 12* has already shown, the explorative analysis unmasks four promising practices from the provider's perspective to manage co-creation in the B2B high-tech domain. The promising practices show various approaches of organizing, designing and structuring the co-creation process of high-tech products. It is noted that described practices are utilized in interplay. They combine into a set of multiple practices used by providers. Furthermore, the interviewees did not present a formal or inclusive approach, but they were capable to describe informally established practices and depict them in a detailed manner. Eventually, it is important to notice that the degree of importance deviates, for instance depending on business relationship already established long-term.

Figure 13 exhibits the findings with *aggregate dimensions* that can be interpreted as promising practices, their associated *2nd order themes* and *1st order concepts*.

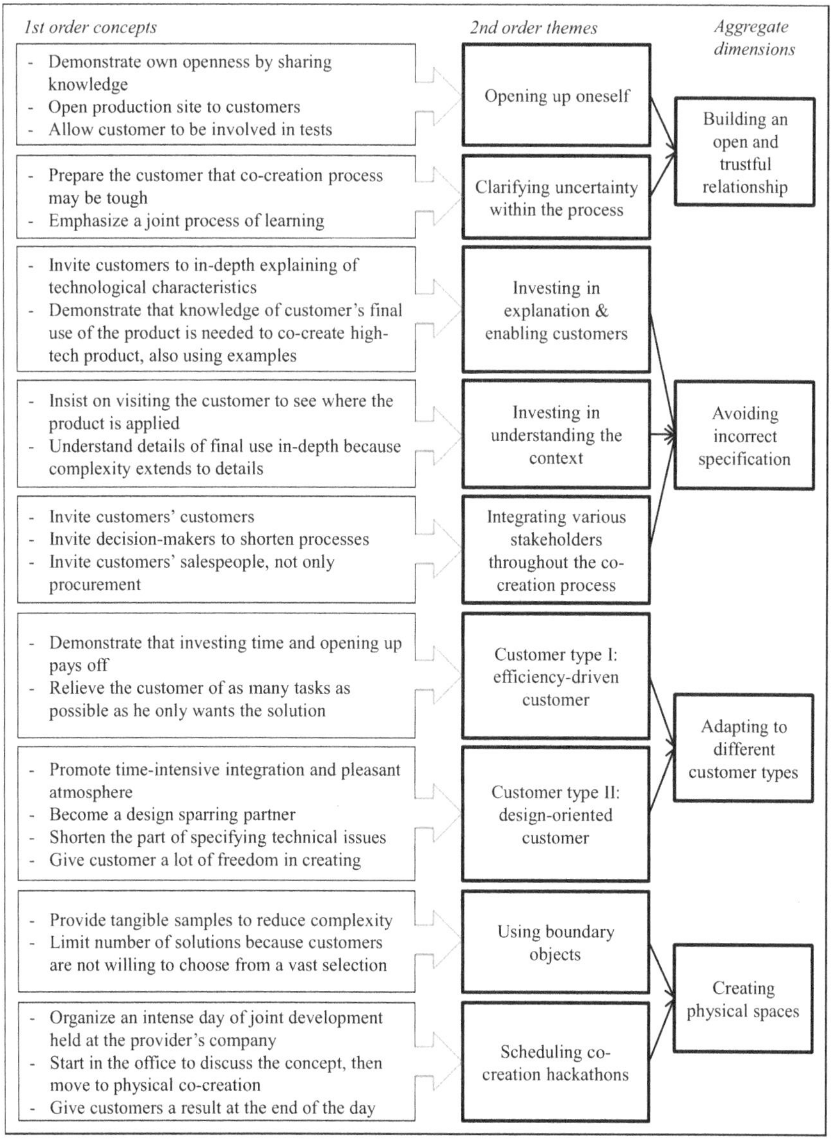

Figure 13: Overview of promising practices for high-tech product co-creation

4.1 Building an open and trustful relationship

The promising practice *building an open and trustful relationship* refers to every action aimed at getting the customer to open up and build trust. This is necessary because providers need customers to deliver precise specifications and also further details to draw a clear picture of customers' requirements. The relevance also stems from the fact that customers may not be able to articulate all their needs due to high levels of sticky information. Other reasons why customers tend not to disclose more information are usually concerns about revealing their own customers or ideas.

To start off, one theme of the practice is labeled *opening up oneself.* Data show that this is crucial for one major reason. Since customers are typically not capable of understanding every detail due to the high complexity, trust is vital for the overall co-creation process. Approaches of opening up include several ways by opening the providing company itself, for instance showing the customer the production site. Goals are to make customers see what the provider is capable of and to build a trustful relationship. Typically, machines and also parameters are not hidden during the production site visit. To put it clearly, the provider demonstrates the openness by sharing own knowledge, or by signaling his willingness to do so[22]:

> *Jonas: "Creating an open, trustful relationship is no trivial matter. You can only do it if you're open yourself. I'm always the first to put openness on the table and say: 'We can talk about everything: pricing, technology, production issues, strategy…' And then I invite him to see my machines and I also show him parameters and stuff like that. I can't do more than that, and often it works."*

> *Horst: "We disclose every single parameter and play with an open hand. There's no easier way to build trust than to share some secret information."*

[22] For all promising practices, *Annex II* contains additional quotes.

The trustful relationship is also built by demonstrating such openness right from the start (Laage-Hellman et al., 2014). Most of the providers, then, share own knowledge and actively stress their willingness for open collaboration to encourage the customer to open up in the same way. This is one approach to face the challenge of customer engagement and requirement capturing, as it supports both challenges alike. Prior (2013) also emphasizes the demonstration of expertise to build the trust in provider's ability and to reduce customer anxiety.

Also at the beginning, providers *clarify uncertainty within the process* in order to prepare the customer for the fact that there is often a high degree of uncertainty. Providers make clear that specifications may not be reached, but that it will be tested together. As such, the co-creation process is labeled as more of a joint learning process:

> *Bert: "At the beginning, we never say it is not possible, we say we must test it. We make it clear that we will test it together, and we tune them [our customers] into this joint process."*

> *Andreas: "We understand it as a learning process with the customer. That's what we stress at the beginning of the process, too."*

This joint learning process is stressed in recent studies from a salesperson perspective (Haas et al., 2012) and also represents an aspect of how customers are integrated into the process. According to the work of Haas et al. (2012), salespeople are required to emphasize the joint process of learning toward the customer. However, it is argued that the primary point of interest is how this learning process is enabled, delivered by the research at hand.

4.2 Avoiding incorrect specification

A major goal of co-creation is to avoid incorrect specifications of the high-tech product, as the close interaction between customer and manufacturer is powerful to elicit customer requirements. This is in line with the challenge of proper requirement capturing described as a major challenge in the context of high-tech product co-creation.

In this vein, one theme is *investing in explanation & enabling customers* to ensure correct specifications. As a result, customers are invited to in-depth explaining of technological characteristics of the high-tech product. This is typically done with a face-to-face meeting:

> *Kerstin: "For the first face-to-face meetings, we invite customers to come to us. It's much easier to explain our products right there in production. We show them every stage of the production process and explain specific features to them. Usually, we can eliminate some uncertainties that would come up later if we didn't do it this way."*

> *Jonas: "We need to get into a casual conversation to figure out his needs and then carefully get him involved that he doesn't, you know, make mistakes in the process."*

In an effort to empower the customer, characteristics and limits are explained in-depth, which is considered time-consuming. However, interviewees stress the importance of face-to-face meetings to elicit customers' needs. Extant literature equally highlights the need for offline interaction when dealing with intricate tasks (Aarikka-Stenroos & Jaakkola, 2012). During the intense explaining and enabling of the customer, providers demonstrate that certain information such as the final use of the product is needed to successfully co-create the high-tech product. Often, the provider uses examples to demonstrate the need for this knowledge:

> *Horst: "From the beginning, the customer must be open and tell us what the application is. This is absolutely essential because only then can we think through every detail."*

> *Gregor: "I just show two samples. One fabric will be a motorcycle seat; the other is for a snowmobile. You know, they look the same but are so different [regarding the technology]. Then I show what happens when it gets hot or cold. We must know the final use; otherwise there are lots of risks."*

This shows how providers address their customers to reveal more information by exemplifying the need. Further, this approach expands customers' understanding of their tasks within the co-creation process (Hohenschwert & Geiger, 2015) and facilitates the elicitation of sticky information from the provider's view (Nordin & Kowalkowski, 2010). Moreover, it enriches the existing factors of openness and willingness to share information (Hohenschwert & Geiger, 2015). Additionally, it is related to defining the core content of the high-tech product (Hakanen & Jaakkola, 2012). Because the literature suggests that customer preferences vary heavily in clarity (Haas et al., 2012), raising awareness for the final use of the product helps tune customers into providing requirements that are as precise as possible.

Moving on to another theme how the provider succeeds in gathering the required specifications for the high-tech product, data shows the theme *investing in understanding the context*. Often, the provider insists on visiting the customer to see the field of application for the product. This allows him to gather relevant details for the high-tech product development:

> *Leif: "The complexity of our products requires one thing: We must go to the customer's site as early as possible. We need to see the area of application, the machines where he will process our fabrics and everything. So it's a lengthy process, of course, but it helps a lot."*

> *Horst: "Incorrect specifications are mainly due to unclear requirements. That hasn't happened for six years now, because when it's not totally clear, we just don't continue the joint development. Usually we notice that early enough."*

If specifications still remain unclear for any reason, or if customers do not reveal requested information, the provider refuses to continue the co-creation process. In other words, the provider is aware of the challenge of incorrect requirement capturing and prefers to not continue the process. In extant research, no similar indications are found.

In general, a move toward *integrating various stakeholders throughout the co-creation process* is observed who have not been involved before: customers of the customer, decision-makers, and the customer's salespeople, which exhibits two major benefits. First, it is found that customer's customers are likely to better express their needs. Second, by inviting marketing, procurement, technical directors, and salespeople, processes are shortened since decisions are made much faster.

> *Björn: "Decision-making has been a major bottleneck especially in the early stage. Now we invite decision-makers, too, because then we really have quick decisions. No checking back or another meeting, it's just done then. Also, we sometimes reach different and even better solutions, going beyond the actual requirement, because the decision-maker comes up with a more farsighted view."*

> *Andreas: "That's what we often do, we ask our customer to bring his customer, because he may better know what he needs, no matter whether it's the creative or engineering guy."*

Overall, this promising practice also sheds light on the challenge of why the co-creation process is time-consuming and tough to manage. At the same time, it adds one aspect to the area of proper customer engagement by showing precisely who else is involved in co-creation. This study extends knowledge with regard to activating relevant actors (Haas et al., 2012) by stating who these actors are.

4.3 Adapting to different customer types

Another interesting practice that was unmasked is that providers adapt to fundamentally different customer types in the co-creation process. This study terms them *efficiency-driven* and *design-oriented customers*. Because their wished degree of involvement differs to a large extent, their engagement requires different approaches.

Looking at *Type I: efficiency-driven customer,* the involvement poses a challenge. Providers often struggle to get this customer type deeply involved in co-creation, as these customers seek for highest efficiency. In line with that, efficiency-driven customers avoid spending much time on the process and want as little involvement as possible. Although providers already try to minimize these customers' involvement, they still need to elicit those customers' needs. So raising that awareness is important. Furthermore, providers demonstrate that the invested time pays off. Nonetheless, such customers are relieved of as many tasks as possible because they only want the high-tech product to solve their problem.

> *Greg: "Some architects didn't want to come to us at the beginning, sure. But once we've convinced them, they won't hesitate to come next time because they recognize that we can drastically shorten the overall development process. They get exactly what they want, so they like to come then."*

> *Carl: "They [customers] don't care whether it's woven or knitted or what coating we use. He just wants a solution for his problem."*

This customer type is seen in line with studies elaborating on the nature of business customers (e. g. Eggert & Ulaga, 2002). More precisely, several studies describe business customers to be driven by efficiency, functional fit and utilitarian value (e. g. Kumar & Grisaffe, 2004; Lapierre, 2000).

The *Type II: design-oriented customer* prefers intense and creative processes. The process is also described as time-intensive and organized in a pleasant atmosphere. It is more akin to becoming a partner for joint design. The work on technological specifications is kept as short as possible, while the work on design issues is intense:

> *Bert: "It's more and more about becoming a design partner in the entire process. They have fun when we react to their ideas and discuss them. That creative part is a major reason why they get involved, I guess. The price issue was never a concern here by the way."*

> *Gabriel: "The customer wants that [investing a lot of time]. He wants to be at our company. He likes to be here and enjoys playing around with different possibilities. Sure, there's a downside: the chemistry has to be right."*

Typically, business customers are described to buy *"for economic rather than emotional reasons"* (Eggert & Ulaga, 2002, p. 109) and another current study suggests that business customers are unlikely to value enjoyment in the process (Vaquero Martín et al., 2016). Interviews, however, strongly emphasize that components such as creative achievement play a role in B2B co-creation. In this regard, literature rather presents indications regarding the degree of involvement. For instance, Jaakkola and Hakanen (2013) found different customer types, one of which prefers heavy involvement – and supports time-intensive processes, in line with the design-oriented type. Another study by Prior (2013) found emotional value to play a role in the customer-provider interaction, but does not emphasize creativity or enjoyment. In terms of the design of the co-creation process, it is easier to get design-oriented customers deeply involved.

Overall, this promising practice shows how different customer types are engaged in very different ways in co-creation. Although extant research gives insight into diverse levels of involvement, data exhibit a bipolarity: two poles are described and labeled. Consequently, from a provider's perspective, two different approaches are used to address the customer types, raising the question of how to identify the type. Data show a rather pragmatic way by asking the customer directly:

> *Andreas: "This depends on the customer. On the one hand you have the creative guy who trusts us with the norms and so on. And then there is the opposite, which means that he pays particular attention to norms and technological issues. Either we notice that anyway, or we just ask directly what he wants when he is at our site. We are just transparent here and ask 'Do we go right or left?'"*

4.4 Creating physical spaces

One theme of the promising practice *creating physical spaces* deals with *using boundary objects*. The latter are essential for reducing complexity and for explaining characteristics of the high-tech product. Especially within the textile industry, samples or tangibles are important due to multisensory experiences. Boundary objects are found to be useful for starting the process with exemplary, high-tech products, since they typically serve as a discussion basis for starting the co-creation process.

> *Carl: "The starting point for new development projects with customers is always a composition of different solutions or designs we offer, and we base our discussion on them."*

> *Anja: "We use 'mood boards' to get a feeling what customers may like. That's a set of possible designs made up individually for each customer meeting in stage zero. Out of these 10 designs, customers choose like one or two, and make adjustments to them, and then we get a notion of what else they like."*

In terms of the process again, it is found that customers are presented with a low number of product designs in order to avoid confusion:

> *Kerstin: "Sure, there is a limit when we present designs to kick-off the process, and that's deliberate. If the customer is given too many options he is only confused in the end. Now it's less options, and I think that helps because it seems much easier to get a notion."*

No other similar indications on this process level of B2B co-creation are found in extant research. However, earlier works stress the importance of boundary objects in such contexts (Carlile, 2002; Star, 1989), while this study provides insight into how and for what purposes they are used in face-to-face settings.

When it comes to the physical framework of the co-creation, the majority of the companies promotes face-to-face settings and has developed one particular approach: they *schedule co-creation hackathons*. Although hackathons are mainly known from the IT context, the database underpins that such approaches are also used in the high-tech domain. This approach is associated to facing the challenge of the time intensity, requirement capturing as well as proper customer engagement. Within the database of this study, the interviewees refer to this as an 'Innovation Day'. The 'Innovation Day' takes place at the production site with testing and prototyping and ideally includes the aforementioned stakeholders (see *4.2 Avoiding incorrect specification; integrating various stakeholders throughout the co-creation process)*. According to the data, this approach is highly promising for co-creating the high-tech product. Typically, the day starts off in the office to discuss the concept on a theoretical level. Then, they move to the production site. Details and limits are explained in front of the machines and throughout the day, and joint testing and prototyping are at the core of this theme. One of the goals is to give the customer a result at the end of the day:

> *Andreas: "The customer should go home and say 'this is my product.' There is somewhat of a relationship, he identifies himself with the product because he feels that he played a role in achieving that success."*

> *Petra: "We try to give the customer like a prototype or something tangible of the co-created product, if possible. It's actually a struggle because in this early stage, we cannot ensure that we could really put this in volume production, but we really think there is a great psychologic effect to give the customer something to take home."*

As such, this practice exhibits a psychological facet that plays a role in the co-creation process, with a striking novelty for the B2B context: it is suggested considering this as commitment and identification with the co-created product. To the author's best knowledge, there are no related indications in extant B2B research.

5 Conclusions

The study in *Part II* was designed to better understand how providers manage and involve business customers in the co-creation process of high-tech products. Grounded in empirical data generated through 29 interviews, four promising practices were unveiled that stretch back to 2nd order themes as well as 1st order concepts which particularly helps showcase single actions used by the provider to manage the co-creation of high-tech products.

It is argued that this study, besides its embedding in the dissertation at hand, entails an individual theoretical contribution, managerial implications and limitations. The following sections depict these areas.

5.1 Theoretical contributions

Taking a problem-solving perspective, *Part II* showed how providers of high-tech products face the ever-greater product complexity by unveiling promising practices for co-creation in this context. Relevant literature was presented also to demonstrate the need for a study on promising practices. Grounded in empirical data with 29 interviews in the German high-tech textile industry, this study unmasked promising practices to co-create high-tech products taking the three main challenges of time intensity, incorrect specification and customer engagement into consideration. Four promising practices show how customers are managed and involved in the co-creation of high-tech products. It is argued for a contribution to the literature in at least four regards.

First, this study contributes to the problem-solving literature (Nickerson & Zenger, 2004) and to the research on sticky information (von Hippel, 1994), as the findings allow for better understanding how a provider of high-tech products can *"generate knowledge that the firm seeks"* (Nickerson & Zenger, 2004, p. 618). By doing so, it also contributes to the literature on the development of new products and services, which is vital for a company's success and an everlasting hotspot in innovation research (Cho & Pucik, 2005; Cooper & Kleinschmidt, 1986). To that conversation, this study adds promising practices of joint product development in the high-tech domain, which is a particularly challenging task (La Rocca et al., 2016; Laage-Hellman et al., 2014; Madhavaram & Appan, 2010). It exhibits the dynamics of innovation practices (Bessant et al., 2003) within a particularly challenging context (La Rocca et al., 2016; Laage-Hellman et al., 2014). The study contributes insight into detailed activities by the provider for joint problem solving in order to co-create high-tech products. With that, the study comes with explanatory power on the topic (Tidd & Bessant, 2018). It is suggested that this clearer picture of current practices helps stimulate the debate of how to design co-creation activities to better face the challenges involved in high-tech product co-creation (Frow et al., 2015; Madhavaram & Appan, 2010; von Hippel, 1994).

Second, it follows calls for further investigations in the field of B2B co-creation research by Kohtamäki and Rajala (2016) and Hohenschwert and Geiger (2015) as well as in the field of high-tech product development by Madhavaram and Appan (2010) and La Rocca et al. (2016). By presenting a range of promising practices, it expands the understanding of where the complexity stems of and how related challenges are managed (Gosling & Naim, 2009). In line with Backman et al. (2007) and Frow et al. (2015), the emphasis is put on actual practices and provides an elaborated picture of how, for instance, a high-tech product hackathon allows to capture the requirements in an efficient way. Specifically, *Part II* moves to a detailed level of these practices and provides insight in how to organize it, e. g. by integrating various stakeholders such as customers' customers and decision-makers into the 'Innovation Day'. Thereby, it answers the question evoked by Haas et al. (2012) who needs to be integrated in B2B co-creation for high-tech products.

Third, properly capturing customer requirements is stressed as a heavy source of failure in innovation management (Hobday & Rush, 1999). Especially in the advent of open innovation, this topic has gained momentum (Enkel, Kausch, & Gassmann, 2005). This study contributes to this conversation as it focuses on co-creation processes with business customers in the high-tech domain. For instance, one unmasked practice delivers approaches how customers are managed in order to *avoid incorrect specifications*, another practice *creating physical spaces* underpins the importance of boundary objects in high-tech product development to diminish risk (Carlile, 2002; Star, 1989). Therefore, it contributes to the risk management in open innovation (Enkel et al., 2005).

Fourth, in contrast to extant studies stating that B2B customers buy *"for economic rather than emotional reasons" (Eggert & Ulaga, 2002, p. 109)*, the exploration identified substantially different customer types in B2B, namely design-oriented and efficiency-driven customers, each of which exhibit different degrees of involvement (Jaakkola & Hakanen, 2013). Especially design-oriented customers seem novel to B2B research as they appear to deeply value enjoyment or creativity within the co-creation process. Akin indications are scant: Prior (2013) emphasizes emotional value to play a role in the customer-provider interaction in B2B, but his findings of emotional value include components such as the reduction of uncertainties or trust in ability. Therefore, it is argued that emotional and social value components in the co-creation process are widely unexplored in extant B2B research. However, one points to the relevance of related works from the B2C context, especially from the mass customization literature (e. g. Merle, Chandon, Roux, & Alizon, 2010).

5.2 Managerial implications

In particular, high-tech companies have to deal with a high degree of product complexity. Specifically, these companies benefit from the promising practices identified in this explorative research. Also, the findings contribute to a company's capability to pursue its ETO business strategy. For practical application, it is argued that the most urgent implications emerge from the distinction between the two customer types for appropriate customer engagement, especially with regard to the two different co-creation processes. For instance, the data show that decreasing direct interaction with efficiency-driven customers has already been informally established, as has the opposite point of intensifying the co-creation process with design-oriented customers. However, efficiency-driven customers need to be involved properly in order to gather requirements, which seems challenging for this type. This is also stressed as a major challenge in current research (Malshe & Friend, 2018). To this end, one promising practice proposes demonstrating the importance of customer's knowledge by giving an example of an incorrect product specification. This approach helps trigger the involvement of customers who are rather unwilling to fulfil their role as co-creators. Further, this also helps face the challenges of requirement capturing and time intensity because it avoids, inter alia, late-discovered requirements.

With regard to managerial implications, this study is not free of industry peculiarities. This emerges mainly from the empirical field, the high-tech textile industry. However, it is argued that the promising practices are likely to hold true for other industries that deal with co-creation of high-tech products. The peculiarity resulting from this study's industry focus may be the use of boundary objects: haptics play a major role in the textile industry, which is assumedly unimportant in machinery, for instance.

5.3 Limitations

Despite the richness of the database, limitations remain. The findings are based on the interviews conducted with actors involved in co-creation from the provider side, which poses twofold limitations. First, the researcher did not have the opportunity to evaluate identified practices in actual co-creation processes in real life, such as using the shadowing technique. Nonetheless, the chosen approach allowed asking questions about the dynamic development of practices developed gradually over time. Moreover, this study was able to derive complexity characteristics by also taking the evolvement over time into consideration, since actors at the heart of dealing with complexity in co-creation for more than ten years were interviewed. These would have remained undetected with a purely ethnographic approach. Second, although practices were mirrored within a workshop after the data analysis with the companies surveyed, this study's results are derived from the provider's perspective. It is a shortcoming of *Part II* to focus only on the provider while dealing with dyadic practices. However, in light of the overall dissertation, the subsequent *Part III* enriches it with customer insight, especially on the bipolarity of customer types in B2B. As B2B research has widely neglected the importance of emotional and social value components within the customer-provider interaction, this represents the most urgent avenue for further research.

Part III – Exploring business customers' value in co-creation

L. K. Grafmüller, *Co-Creation of High-Tech Products in the B2B Domain*,
Markt- und Unternehmensentwicklung Markets and Organisations,
https://doi.org/10.1007/978-3-658-28412-1_3

1 Needs and objectives[23]

> *"Finally, there is the most difficult question: 'What does the customer consider value?'"* (Drucker, 1954, p. 47)

After analyzing the provider's perspective in *Part II*, this part is dedicated to the customers' domain. Thereby, the studies on the dyadic co-creation process are complemented by the customers' view. *Part III* picks up the second research gap and examines the customer value of the co-creation process (see *Part I; 2.4 Research gaps and needs*). It is embedded in the dissertation as shown in *Figure 14*:

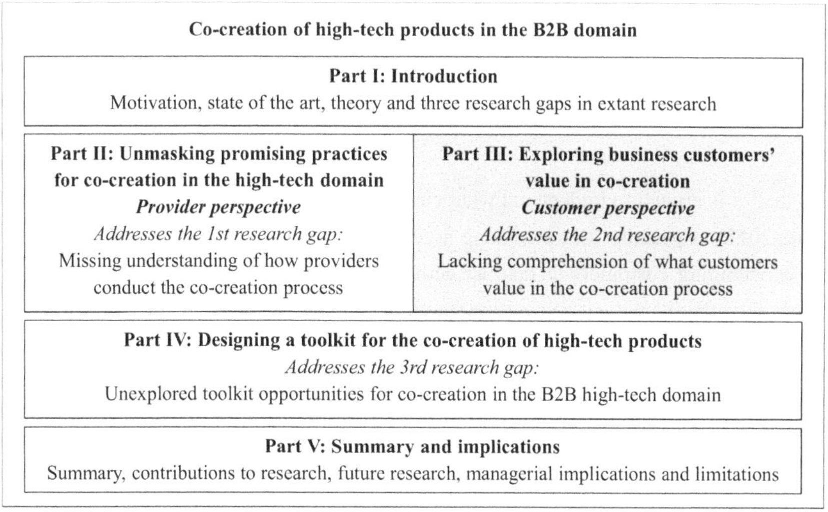

Figure 14: Embedding of *Part III* in the dissertation

[23] Earlier versions of this study have been presented at the 2016 *7th International Conference on Mass Customization and Personalization in Central Europe, Novi Sad, Serbia*, as well as at the doctoral colloquium of *The 2017 World Mass Customization & Personalization Conference*, Aachen, Germany. All publications of the author are listed in Annex I. An updated version of this research is prepared for journal publication with the authors Grafmüller, Velamuri, & Möslein.

In the following paragraphs, this study is motivated more detailed and the research question to target the second research gap is derived (see *Figure 14*).

As one central topic in innovation and business management research for more than 40 years (Cross, 1972; Mustak et al., 2013; Perks et al., 2012; Piller et al., 2011), it has been shown that customer integration into joint development processes for high-tech products is a tough challenge (Jacob, 2006; La Rocca et al., 2016; Malshe & Friend, 2018). One of the goals of co-creation is to elicit sticky information (von Hippel, 1994), which is requirements that customers are not able to articulate (Nordin & Kowalkowski, 2010; Tuli et al., 2007). While more and more B2B companies integrate customers in innovation activities for co-creating high-tech products (La Rocca et al., 2016; Laage-Hellman et al., 2014; Malshe & Friend, 2018), the growing body of literature emphasizes the role of properly designed co-creation processes along the customer preferences (Frow et al., 2015; Harmancioglu et al., 2007; Hienerth & Lettl, 2011; Malshe & Friend, 2018; Vaquero Martín et al., 2016).

For that, it is crucial to understand what customers value during such processes (Frow et al., 2015), especially for co-creating high-tech products (La Rocca et al., 2016) and for encouraging customers to take an active role (Malshe & Friend, 2018). In other words, the effectiveness of co-creation stands and falls with customer engagement (Hienerth & Lettl, 2011; Roberts et al., 2014). In line with this, the increasing focus on the customer's role in co-creation processes brings according questions to the fore (Malshe & Friend, 2018; Randhawa et al., 2016).

Looking at customer value in B2B, the predominant credo in research describes business customers to *"buy for economic rather than emotional reasons"* (Eggert & Ulaga, 2002, p. 109). In line with that, business customers are described to value efficiency, speed and quick responses, i. e. *functional* value (e. g. Gordon et al., 1993; Lapierre, 1997). Looking at value components besides that, for instance Füller et al. (2010) detail that the appropriateness of an experience-driven co-creation process is rather doubtful for the B2B context. As one major reason, they stress that business customers source strategically, maximizing profits and negotiating over long-term commitments. Further, they argue that products are highly embedded in the organization, which strongly influences the co-creation process, as many more attributes need to be considered. In conclusion, they state that the *"customer motivation and ability to engage"* is key for successful co-creation (ibid., p. 1377). Another point is made by Vaquero Martín et al. (2016), setting out that industrial purchasers – hence business customers – are typically not the users of the product. Therefore, it is found likely that they need to be engaged in an efficiency-driven way.

However, recent research also indicates the relevance of *emotional* and *social* value components in the B2B context (Arslanagic-Kalajdzic & Zabkar, 2017; Prior, 2013). Moreover, Hakanen and Jaakkola (2012) describe one camp of business customers that wishes deep involvement, which is argued to be another indication for emotional and social value, as this is hard to explain with merely functional value. Also, a recent study by Malshe and Friend (2018) delivers evidence on 'non-receptive customers' in a B2B setting. The authors revealed that several business customers are reluctant when co-creation is initiated. In other terms, from time to time, business customers are unwilling to participate in co-creation processes, which threatens the co-creation success (Cui & Wu, 2017; Malshe & Friend, 2018).

Taking a problem-solving perspective, this unwillingness from the customers means that the provider struggles to engage them into the joint problem solving, which discourages the provider to elicit the sticky information (Nickerson & Zenger, 2004; von Hippel, 1994). As a consequence, for successful problem solving the customer must be engaged by understanding his perceived value within the co-creation process.

As emotional and social value components in the B2B domain require a better understanding (Arslanagic-Kalajdzic & Zabkar, 2017; Prior, 2013), this study is dedicated to examine this topic; for which the end consumer context is much more advanced (Füller et al., 2011; Merle et al., 2010). A clearer picture promises an improvement on B2B co-creation processes (Madhavaram & Appan, 2010) and follows several calls for further action (La Rocca et al., 2016; Laage-Hellman et al., 2014; Malshe & Friend, 2018; Vaquero Martín et al., 2016). More precisely, for instance, a recent literature review on customer participation in co-creating offerings by Mustak et al. (2013) stresses that customer value must be understood to manage the co-creation process accordingly.

In the light of the second research gap, the customer value in the co-creation of high-tech products is at the center of interest. It is acknowledged that studies on functional value are well-advanced, while research on social and emotional value is both scant and required to properly design the co-creation process with business customers. Bearing primarily on Prior's (2013) seminal work on emotional and social value in B2B, *Part III* seeks to answer the question to target the second research gap:

> *RQ to address the second research gap:*
> *What emotional and social value components play a role in B2B co-creation with high product complexity?*

An explorative research design was chosen to uncover and better understand components of emotional and social value. 42 semi-structured interviews were conducted with customer co-creators in the German textile industry. Because technical expertise is needed, co-creators from the customer side come typically with an engineering background to this industry. All interviewees work in SMEs, acknowledged for adopting open innovation activities effectively (Spithoven et al., 2013) and early (Hochleitner et al., 2016). In line with calls for research, customers were inquired as it is aimed for unmasking value components from the customer domain (Mustak et al., 2013; Petri & Jacob, 2016; Randhawa et al., 2016).

In contrast to the predominant credo in extant research, the findings underpin the importance of emotional and social value components in B2B co-creation processes. The explorative study reveals three value components: *openness* from the provider is prerequisite for co-creating high-tech products, *playfulness* relates to customers' desire to play with different technologies which does not necessarily correspond with the actual goal, and *self-fulfillment* refers to customers' emotional satisfaction and pride in contributing to the high-tech product. From the existence of such value components in B2B co-creation emerges a profound implication regarding novel designs of the co-creation process. The conclusion outlines limitations and construes the need for further research.

This empirical study constitutes *Part III* of the dissertation and contains five *chapters*. *Chapter 2* draws on the relevant literature in the areas of value in B2B research and co-creation in the industrial context. Afterwards, *Chapter 3* illuminates the research design by detailing the sampling, data collection, and data analysis. *Chapter 4* presents the findings. Finally, *Chapter 5* derives contributions to research, managerial implications and avenues for further research.

2 Theoretical underpinning

Chapter 2 sets out the theoretical underpinning for this study by first defining perceived customer value. Then, related work on the importance of understanding it in co-creation is presented through a problem-solving lens. It concludes by a review of customer value on B2B co-creation.

2.1 Perceived customer value

To date, understanding customer value has been an enduring quest (Drucker, 1954, p. 46; Holbrook, 1994; Roberts et al., 2014). B2B research has been heavily concerned with according questions (Eggert & Ulaga, 2002; Gil-Saura, Frasquet-Deltoro, & Cervera-Taulet, 2009; Lapierre, 2000).

As this study aims to understand the role of emotional and social value components in B2B co-creation, the concept of value is defined. This study follows Flint, Woodruff, and Gardial (1997), stating that *"value is created by delivering benefits that help customers achieve their goals"* (ibid., p. 168). Also, value is defined as a trade-off between benefits and sacrifices, which depends on each perception (Zeithaml, 1988). Kortge and Okonkwo (1993) stress the subjectivity of the conception of *perceived customer value*: identical products or processes are perceived in different ways by different customers. This study is concerned with the latter understanding. Consequently, when referred to value, it is touched upon the concept of perceived customer value. The value components this study aims at unfold in co-creation processes, in which high-tech products are co-created in a customer-provider interaction.

2.2 Sticky information and customer value in co-creation

As the degree of customer involvement in co-creation is constantly growing (Laage-Hellman et al., 2014), the proper engagement of customers becomes more and more important to capture customer's requirements. While a great majority of extant articles has dealt with the nature of co-creation (Malshe & Friend, 2018; Mustak et al., 2013;

Roberts et al., 2014), the motives and values of how to engage customers in such processes have been rather absent.

However, it is decisive to understand what values motivate customers to deeply engage in joint development processes, and how they are motivated throughout the entire process (Füller et al., 2010; Roberts et al., 2014). A better comprehension of according questions *"enable[s] firms to strategically manage their interactions in a way that creates superior value [for the customer] and for the firm itself (e. g. superior wealth and growth)"* (Roberts et al., 2014, p. 147). Several studies call for that in this area, as an understanding of customer value in co-creation processes is crucially important to its success (La Rocca et al., 2016; Malshe & Friend, 2018; Mustak et al., 2013; Roberts et al., 2014).

Also the problem-solving perspective helps discover why it is important to understand what customers value in co-creation. Through that lens, problem-solving activities need to be properly designed by the provider (Nickerson & Zenger, 2004) in order to successfully engage customers. Therefore, the problem-solving success depends on customer's motivation to contribute valuable knowledge for the company (Nickerson & Zenger, 2004). To put it in the context of co-creation, the knowledge that a company seeks by means of co-creation is the sticky information (von Hippel, 1994). Hence, in order to capture sticky information, it is decisive to acknowledge the importance of considering the customer value within the co-creation process (Nickerson & Zenger, 2004).

2.3 Extant research on customer value in B2B co-creation

The topic of customer value has been heavily discussed in B2B research (Anderson & Narus, 1998; Eggert & Ulaga, 2002; Ulaga, 2001). The credo in related studies follows Eggert and Ulaga (2002) who state that business customers buy for economic, not emotional reasons. Nonetheless, recent studies point to both the existence and importance of emotional and social value in B2B co-creation. The subsequent *sub-sections* exhibit the literature on *functional value, social value* and *emotional value* in B2B research. As stated above, the area of *functional value* draws a rather elaborated picture.

Functional value. B2B research suggests that business customers generally buy for economic, not emotional reasons (Eggert & Ulaga, 2002). They are described to value efficiency, speed and quick responses, i. e. functional value components (e. g. Gordon et al., 1993; Lapierre, 1997). Functional value is derived from solving a problem through functional, physical or utilitarian attributes (Prior, 2013). A picture in this respect, which is a single dimension of value components, is drawn by a large number of studies. An overview is presented in *Table 7*. Focusing on process-related value components that unfold throughout the co-creation process (Aarikka-Stenroos & Jaakkola, 2012), this study especially bears on relevant studies from the innovation management and industrial marketing domain, touching upon the research areas of relationship marketing, perceived value in B2B and co-creation in the industrial context.

Table 7: Functional value components in the co-creation process for high-tech products

Value component	Description	Sources
The degree of definition and communication of requirements	Increasing degrees of both increase likelihood of achieving desired objective	Hawkins, Gravier, Berkowitz, and Muir (2015), Ulaga (2003), Nordin and Kowalkowski (2010)
Moderation of the co-creation process by the provider	Appropriate organization and moderation benefits the efficiency	La Rocca et al. (2016), Petri and Jacob (2016), Vaquero Martín et al. (2016)
Flexibility within the process	Strict formalization of the process negatively impacts salespeople's value opportunity recognition	Kumar and Grisaffe (2004), Prior (2013), Ulaga (2003), Ulaga and Eggert (2005), Lapierre (2000), Vaquero Martín et al. (2016)
Speed, efficiency value, responsiveness & easy access value	Whole process as efficient and fast as possible regarding information processing, incoming inspections or order-handling	Gordon et al. (1993), Kumar and Grisaffe (2004), Prior (2013), Ulaga and Eggert (2005), Lapierre (2000)
Expert consulting value	Customers value strong expertise, also about the customer's needs.	Eggert, Ulaga, and Schultz (2006), Fauska et al. (2014), Aarikka-Stenroos and Jaakkola (2012)
Offline interaction value	Strong need for offline interaction due to high complexity (e. g. intangible product characteristics)	Eggert et al. (2006), Fauska et al. (2014), Prior (2013), Vaquero Martín et al. (2016)

Given that functional dimension of value components, it might seem obvious how to design co-creation processes for high-tech products, but recent studies hold indications that this is not sufficient. For instance, several studies emphasize different levels of involvement that is wished by the business customer in co-creation processes (Hakanen & Jaakkola, 2012; Jaakkola & Hakanen, 2013). Different customer types regarding their co-creation process preferences are described: while some customers wish deep involvement, the others prefer it *"to be kept to a minimum"* (Jaakkola & Hakanen, 2013, p. 53). The latter customer type is suggested to be efficiency-driven (e. g. Gordon et al., 1993; Ulaga & Eggert, 2005). The other camp, the deeply involved customer type, arguably needs to be addressed with other value components than described in the B2B literature listed. Moreover, Aarikka-Stenroos and Jaakkola (2012) found that the perceived value is not only related to the delivered solution, but that it is also generated through the co-creation process itself. More precise insight is delivered by Prior (2013): he found additional dimensions of value in B2B co-creation processes, namely *social* and *emotional* value, which is depicted in the following *sections.*

Social value. As indicated, a number of recent studies draws attention to other dimensions of value components in B2B besides the functional ones (Arslanagic-Kalajdzic & Zabkar, 2017; Candi & Kahn, 2016; Prior, 2013). Triggering this conversation, Prior (2013) investigated the link between the activities of supplier representatives and the effects of customer perceived value in complex industrial solutions. In this context of intense interactions between supplier and customer, he found multi-dimensional sources of intangible value and stresses the importance of *social* and *emotional* value components within the process. Social value relates to *"an improvement in social status or positive feedback from members of the individual's major social reference groups"* (ibid., p. 1194). Prior (2013) categorizes, for instance, *efficiency* as a *functional* value component, which is in line with a series of early studies (e. g. Gordon et al., 1993; Ulaga & Eggert, 2005). *Social* value components include *professional execution* and *trust in ability.* The topic of trust is also stressed in other studies, more precisely it represents a precursor for successful joint projects. In other words, effective co-creation is only established after building a trustful relationship (Laage-Hellman et al., 2014; Leseure, 2015).

Emotional value. Also in the empirical study of Prior (2013), *emotional* value is described in the B2B domain, which is considered rather striking. Emotional value encompasses, inter alia, *trust in ability* due to high complexity as well as *reduced customer anxiety*. It is defined as follows: *"[e]motional value arises through incidents where the individual experiences positive feelings such as happiness, joy and satisfaction"* (ibid., p. 1194). The study suggests that, although B2B research has drawn another picture thus far, *"the appraisal of value in complex industrial solutions is not always a rational process"* (Prior, 2013, p. 1199). Adopting Prior's multi-dimensional value approach for different contexts, Arslanagic-Kalajdzic and Zabkar (2017) and Candi and Kahn (2016) state that consumer research is much more advanced in the conceptualization of value than research on business customers. It is specified that value as a multi-dimensional concept is empirically validated in B2C settings. Indeed, in end consumer settings, co-creation has gained particular attention over the last decade in innovation research (Füller et al., 2011; Merle et al., 2010; Sanders & Stappers, 2008). For instance, for B2C, Füller et al. (2011) deliver evidence what impact creative experience on the co-creation quality has, or Merle et al. (2010) describe such emotional value components such as creativity and enjoyment in a consumer context.

Given these arguments, it is argued for a strong and justified need for studying in-depth the emotional and social value components in B2B co-creation processes that involve high product complexity.

3 Method and data

This *chapter* outlines the method and data of the second empirical study. The *research approach* in the first *section* depicts the research design. The latter is then detailed in the second *section* with the sampling, data collection as well as data analysis.

3.1 Research approach

Part III targets the question what emotional and social value components play a role in B2B co-creation for customers. The overall context for this question is described in *Part I* and deeper explained in the latter *sections* of *Part III*. As shown, extant B2B research typically takes a provider's rather than the customers' perspective (Mustak et al., 2013). Thus, this study focuses on the neglected customer domain (Payne et al., 2008; Petri & Jacob, 2016; Tuli et al., 2007). With the goal to deeper investigate emotional and social value, a qualitative research approach appears expedient to elicit the customer's perceived value. This is because the qualitative approach also allows for delving *"beneath the surface to explore issues that are [...] implicit"* (Tracy, 2010, p. 843). This seems particularly helpful for investigating the rather abstract concept of perceived value. Especially, the qualitative approach allows for asking *how* and *what* questions, and for making the study participant elaborate freely on open questions related to the topic under investigation (Eisenhardt, 1989). Thus, the interview study is based on a series of open questions that also aim to elicit customer value in an implicit way, for which the qualitative research paradigm is argued to be particularly suitable; for instance, customers were supposed to describe critical incidents within experienced co-creation processes. By doing so, it is possible to ground the findings on implicit statements and to put them into context.

With its focus on value components from a customer perspective in high-tech product co-creation, *Part III* aims at unveiling social and emotional value. The interview study builds on interviews with customer co-creators from the German high-tech textile industry who are frequently involved in co-creating high-tech products.

3.2 Sample and data

Especially technology experts in niche markets are concerned with co-creating high-tech products (Teirlinck & Spithoven, 2013). Their business heavily relies on their expertise. In this context, this study was conducted in the East German high-tech textile industry[24]. For the purposes of this study, buyers from manufacturers of furniture fabrics were inquired in their role as customers. Their companies offer textiles with specific functions for outdoor use such as waterproof and tear-proof, or produce coated fabrics and textile equipment as well as technical textiles. The interview database, also exposing the companies the interviewees work for, are showcased in *Table 8* with more details.

The main sampling criterion for the selection of the interviewees was to include customers often and deeply involved in co-creation processes. Moreover, it was sought to include several customers of the providers inquired in *Part II*. In total, 19 out of the 42 interviews of this study represent customers of the providers interviewed in the first empirical study. For all interviewees, purposeful sampling was used (Patton, 1990) involving technical directors, sales representatives, development and procurement managers as well as CEOs. This served to gain insights into the concept of emotional value components from different angles. Especially in smaller companies, CEOs themselves are involved by other companies in high-tech co-creation, as they also fulfil the role of industrial buyers. All interviewees come with an engineering background. The interviews were scheduled for one hour, the shortest was 49 min. An overview of the interviewees with their different branches as well as companies, lengths of the individual interviews and positions of the interviewees are exposed in *Table 8*. All interviews were conducted in German, transcribed and then analyzed. The quotes in this study were translated by a professional translator.

[24] A description of the context of this research with examples is provided in *Part I, Chapter 3*.

Table 8: Overview of sample and interview database of *Part III*

Industry sector	Firm	Brief description	Interviews	Interview length	Position of interviewee	Staff
Furniture fabrics	Furn_1	Manufacturer of outdoor furniture with specific functions for, e. g., water-proof, tear-proof	4	4h 14 min	Technical Director, 3x Procurement Manager	125
	Furni_2	Processor of fabrics with specific functions for indoor use, e. g., acoustic insulating and fireproof	3	2h 48 min	CEO, Technical Director, Sales Manager	50
	Furn_3	High-quality fabric manufacturer with specific functions for indoor use, e. g., acoustic & heat insulating, fireproof	4	3h 58 min	CEO, 2x Procurement Manager, Development Manager	75
	Furn_4	High-quality fabric manufacturer with specific functions for indoor use, e. g., acoustic & heat insulating, fireproof	2	2h 30 min	CEO, Technical Director	25
Coated fabrics & textile equipment	Coated_1	Manufacturer of coated fabrics with specific functions, e. g., tear-proof, heat-resistant, cold-resistant, embossment	4	4h 01 min	CEO, Head of Development, 2x Procurement Manager	150
	Coated_2	Processor of coated fabrics with specific functions, e. g., heat-resistant, cold-resistant, resilience	2	2h 10 min	CEO, Technical Director	50
	Coated_3	Manufacturer of coated fabrics with specific functions, e. g., heat-resistant, cold-resistant, resilience	1	1h 04 min	CEO	25
	Coated_4	Service provider for coated fabrics, adding specific functions, e. g., soft hand, impregnation	2	1h 55 min	CEO, Development Manager	25
	Coated_5	Service provider for coated fabrics, adding specific functions, e. g., soft hand, biocidal treatment	3	3h 11 min	CEO, Technical Director Procurement Manager	50
Technical textiles	Tech_1	Manufacturer of yarn for technical textiles with specific functions, e. g., tensile strength, heat- & cold-resistant	4	3h 58 min	CEO, Sales Manager, Technical Director, Procurement Manager	100
	Tech_2	Manufacturer of lightweight non-wovens with specific functions, e. g., acoustic & heat insulating	5	4h 26 min	Technical Director, Head of Technology, 3x Procurer	200
	Tech_3	Manufacturer of non-wovens with specific functions, e. g., acoustic & heat insulating	1	1h 15 min	CEO	25
	Tech_4	Service provider for technical textiles, adding specific functions, e. g., biocidal treatment, impregnation	2	2h 03 min	Procurement Manager, Sales Manager	100
	Tech_5	Service provider for technical textiles, adding specific functions, e. g., water-resistant, fireproof	2	2h 12 min	Procurement Manager, Technical Director	100
	Tech_6	Service provider for technical textiles, adding specific functions, e. g., water-resistant, fireproof	3	2h 53 min	CEO, Technical Director, Procurement Manager	125
In total			**42**	**42h 38 min**		

The semi-structured interviews were conducted face-to-face during on-site visits. In total, 42 interviews were conducted to shed light on the customer's perspective on the value of the co-creation process. The database encompasses interview material of 42 hours 38 minutes in total, all audiotaped and transcribed. The database is considered both thick and rich as it represents a rather large database with deep nuances. Data gathering was not only stopped when data saturation was reached, but when intricate phenomena were deeply explained by various interviewees (Fusch & Ness, 2015).

To explore business customers' social and emotional value in co-creation, semi-structured interviews were employed. The interview guide was based on a series of topics drawn from the literature (see *Table 9*), following Yin (2014, p. 69). It was particularly sought to make the interviewee elaborate on his perception of the co-creation process. Interviewees were supposed to describe in-depth how they experience the overall process and to detail every nuance of the process. The personal interviews took place as follows.

After a short introduction of the interviewee and his position, he was asked to explain how typical co-creation processes are initiated, organized and structured, and how they perceive the joint development process. Particularly, the interviewee was supposed to describe it in a sequential way. Depending on the degree of detailedness, queries concerned deeper descriptions of single actions, or process-related perceptions of the interviewee as the interviewees with engineering background often tended to move to technical issues. Then, interviewees were asked for good and bad anecdotes they experienced in co-creation processes, which is powerful to elicit *critical incidents* within the process (Flanagan, 1954). A critical incident in this study is, e. g., an action by the provider that jeopardizes the co-creation success, or vice-versa an action that spurs the process. This is argued to be suitable because interviewees elaborate on motivators – and values – to properly engage them in co-creation processes. After this, interviewees answered a series of open questions (see *Table 9*), accompanied by follow-up queries whenever necessary.

Overall, it was sought to unveil emotional and social value in an implicit way, drawing on deep process descriptions from a customer's view and eventually more targeted questions. This procedure was initially tested with a handful of interviewees and then improved throughout the process (Miles et al., 2014), using the constant comparative method by Glaser (1965). In order to ensure the appropriateness of data interpretation, first results were discussed with customers. The interview guideline encompasses two building blocks, distinguished by actual experiences by the interviewee and an exemplary co-creation process, shown in *Table 9*:

Table 9: Interview guideline of *Part III*

Objective	Questions
1. In-depth description of co-creation processes	From your perspective, please describe a co-creation process with all details! How are you involved, (Piller et al., 2011), and especially how is complexity and uncertainty faced? (La Rocca et al., 2016) How are co-creation processes structured, and how do you perceive the different phases? When thinking about co-creation processes that you experienced, what are good/best and bad/worst experiences? Please elaborate on critical (both positive and negative) incidents! (Flanagan, 1954) How have you been demotivated and motivated? (Roberts et al., 2014)
2. Elaboration on an exemplary co-creation process	What is an ideal design of a co-creation process from your perspective? What means are needed by the provider to engage you? (Hakanen & Jaakkola, 2012) What drives you to deeply engage in the process? (Mustak et al., 2013; Prior, 2013) What discourages you to engage in the process? (Hakanen & Jaakkola, 2012) Please delineate an ideal co-creation process, from start to finish!

Follow-up queries asked *why* questions for deeper descriptions of single actions and process-related perceptions of the interviewee.

3.3 Data analysis

The qualitative content analysis followed Corbin and Strauss (2008), and the interviews were coded using the QDA software ATLAS.ti. (Gioia et al., 2013; Mason, 2002). Both deductive and inductive elements were combined in a two-step process (Miles et al., 2014).

Starting with the inductive part, the first step included the marking of emotional and social value components related to the co-creation process, as the existence of such value components has been known from extant research (e. g. Prior, 2013). Then, inductively, the coder developed sub-categories for the codes *emotional* and/or *social value*. Thereby, constructs drawn from the literature as well as exploring new constructs were at the core of the analysis process. Grounded in the database, deductive and inductive elements of qualitative research are thus combined (Miles et al., 2014). For instance, interviewees described one emotional component, analogously: *"I like to play sometimes with different technologies because it's fun"*; the coder labeled the segment *importance of fun.*

In the second step, then, codes were aligned terminologically, also the different sub-categories, and the code list was revised (Corbin & Strauss, 2008; Miles et al., 2014). For the given example, *playfulness* was chosen as this captures both the notion of having fun as well as the sense of emotional satisfaction through the co-creation process. With a revised code list, the subsequent analysis part condensed the data and patterns within the database to shed light on the different facets of the explored value components. Overall, the database encompasses the quotes and sub-categories described in *Figure 15* that was set up with the coding software ATLAS.ti. The numbers behind the terms exhibit the underlying, coded segments grounded in the 42 interviews. The findings are presented in the subsequent *chapter* more in detail.

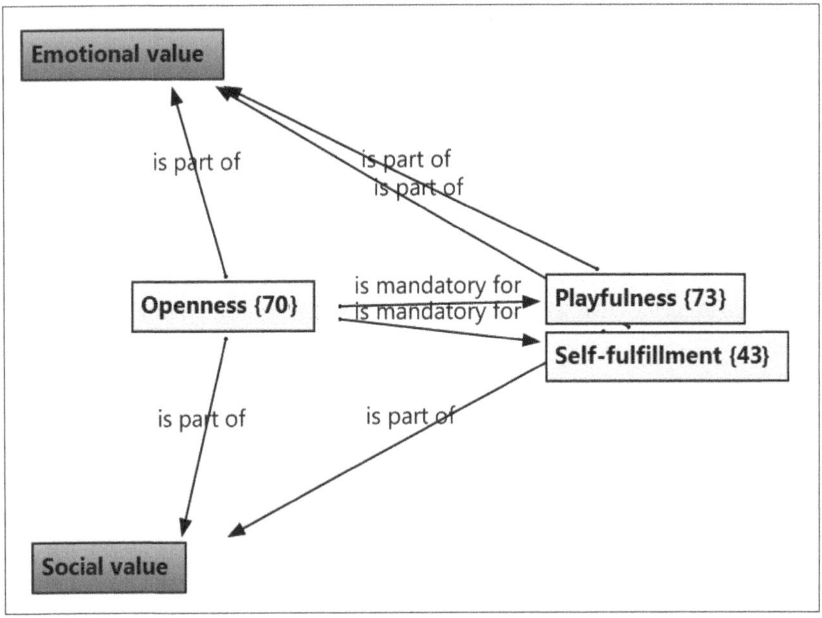

Figure 15: Overview of codes for social and emotional value in B2B co-creation

4 Findings

After setting the stage with the theoretical underpinnings and the research design, this *chapter* presents the findings from the explorative study. It encompasses the findings of analyzing customer value components in co-creation processes with high product complexity. The focus of the findings chapter is explicitly placed on the areas of emotional and social value components, exploring a field that has been widely neglected in previous B2B studies (Arslanagic-Kalajdzic & Zabkar, 2017; Prior, 2013). The analysis reveals three value components on the dimensions of emotional and social value, which are discussed in light of extant literature.

Before moving on, one central point concerns the conceptualization of business customers. Although business customers are usually seen as companies, the co-creation process is conducted by individuals who act on behalf of their organization (Baumann & Le Meunier-FitzHugh, 2014). The company representatives who represent the business customer enter the process based on their organizational roles and personal characteristics. As a consequence, it is acknowledged that it is dealt with different individuals with different preferences, that are engaged in the co-creation process (Perks et al., 2012).

Overall, this study identified two camps of representatives who exhibit substantial differences with respect to expectations as well as the form and level of involvement in the co-creation process. The following quote overarches the database of the 42 interviews:

> *Bert: "From my experience, there are two [customer] types in co-creation projects. One customer only focuses on the 'job to be done' and wants to be as efficient as possible. He just wants his problem to be solved. The other guy is like me: It's the creative guy. I usually enjoy the joint development with experts from other companies, it feels like much fun rather than working!"*

Data suggest separating two different customer groups: efficiency-driven and design-oriented customers. The major difference is that efficiency-driven customers are particularly satisfied by functional value components, while design-oriented customers especially value emotional and social components in the co-creation process. Consequently, this explorative study is primarily concerned with the design-oriented type.

The term design-oriented is, by far, not limited to aesthetics, but touches upon the design of a high-tech product in terms of feasibility, functionality or technological innovativeness. This main finding better explains the different degrees of involvement estimated by two different customer types described by Jaakkola and Hakanen (2013) and Hakanen and Jaakkola (2012). Before diving deeper, *Table 10* gives an overview of the findings derived from the 42 interviews. Afterwards, these value components are described in more detail.

Table 10: Findings on emotional and social value in B2B co-creation of high-tech products

Value component	Dimension	Description
Openness	emotional/social	*Openness describes the customers' demand of the provider to be open.*
Playfulness	emotional/social	*Playfulness relates to customers' desire to play with different technologies, which does not necessarily correspond with the actual goal.*
Self-fulfillment	emotional	*Self-fulfillment describes customers' emotional satisfaction and pride in contributing to the development of a novel, high-tech product.*

4.1 Openness

Openness describes the customers' demand of the provider to be open. The analysis suggests that this value component, assigned to both the emotional and social dimension, plays a crucial role in co-creating high-tech products. Being in mandatory relation to the *playfulness* and *self-fulfillment,* it paves the way for a successful co-creation process in the first place (see *Figure 15*). Dealing with a high-tech industry, *openness* is heavily stressed in the data for which several reasons were identified. As an initial example, the customer often wishes a company inspection to assess whether the provider is capable of handling the technology. Thereby, *openness* is explicitly underlined by the customer as a precursor for co-creating high-tech products:

> *Janko: „I must see the company. I must see their machines and get a feeling for their capabilities and so on. Of course, there are always issues when I say that I want to see their production because the company immediately thinks of disclosure issues. But if a company finds a way and is that open and shows me their machinery, they will have me contributing in high-tech projects."*

> *Jürgen: "For the first personal meetings, I prefer going to the supplier. Ideally, they show me their site and I can touch and feel what technologies they master."*

In total, *openness* exhibits two facets, namely the *appropriateness of the provider himself to open up* in the co-creation process and the *enabling the customer*. The following paragraphs detail these findings.

Appropriateness of the provider himself to open up. Co-creation processes for high-tech products represent an intense customer-provider interaction. During that, the parties involved exchange a lot of information. As parts of that information are considered confidential or critical, the disclosure is perceived as a balancing act. If the provider does not open up himself, the customer is unlikely to open up either. With the words from interviewed customers, the provider must find an appropriate degree of opening up:

> *Michael: "Generally, the providing company must be as open as possible and also reveal knowledge, as I do the same, especially in joint high-tech projects. Otherwise I get the feeling they just exploit my expertise."*

> *Benno: "There must be an open and trustful relationship for a successful collaboration. Because, in the end, we deal with tons of knowledge that we could not manage with an NDA [non-disclosure agreement]."*

Although this task runs into danger of a chicken-and-egg dilemma, evoking the question who makes the first move, data suggest that typically the provider is in charge of the initiation, in line with current research that takes a provider's view (Aarikka-Stenroos & Jaakkola, 2012). Also, interviewees stress the importance of a trustful relationship to co-create successfully because this permits to focus the efforts on the actual project rather than on side issues. It is argued that this is equally within the context of *openness*:

> *Holger: "Finding into a casual conversation is key for developing together. It is a relief when you can blank out all the other issues and get concentrated on the project only. The leading company must take care of that in an open environment and exclude anything that could hinder us [the customers] to frankly work with them."*

Accordingly, it is the provider's task to eliminate factors that distract the co-creation process to allow for better focusing. There is a close connection to the studies by Leseure (2015) and Laage-Hellman et al. (2014), considering a trustful relationship mandatory for successful co-creation. Overall, regarding the facet *appropriateness of the provider himself to open up,* interviewees assign its responsibility to the provider as he conducts the entire process, in line with current research that merely considers the provider's view (La Rocca et al., 2016).

Enabling the customer. Nearly all interviewees stress the importance of customer enabling in the co-creation process as a founding block of the value component *openness*. Due to high product complexity, this facet mainly concerns the technological level to enable the customer to make right choices for his particular needs, for which the provider must exhibit a considerable level of *openness*. This is found crucial in high-tech product development as the customer benefits from working with experts in this domain. In addition, the technologically-based enabling theme was found throughout the entire process.

Gregor: "There are so many technologies and fields of expertise only in coating. If I invest my time, I want to be explained that stuff and learn a lot myself."

The topic of enabling is mainly achieved by a motivated, engaging and committed provider with an open mindset. Customers seek to assess that commitment and motivation to enable them already in an early phase. Moreover, data highlight that signaling the commitment for enabling is considered a major reason to choose a particular provider for co-creating high-tech products:

Sascha: "I often failed finding a supplier that engages in a proper collaboration. I notice that right at the beginning when he doesn't try to understand my specific case. I always wondered [...] how they want to co-create a product with us without asking where we would use it in the end, what solution is currently in place and so on. He [the provider] is the expert, he has the overview. He must adapt the process to my level of knowledge and start at this point."

Regarding this constant adaption of the process, the explorative study also suggests that this enabling requires cautious guidance within an open environment, because customers bring in unfeasible ideas in technological regards relatively often. Here, the interviewed customers emphasize a careful reaction and a kind absorption of the idea:

Anja: "I know that some of my ideas may be stupid as I cannot be an expert in any field here. But then it depends on the company how they enable me to make 'good' contributions. I think the topic of enabling is critical when I'm involved in complex product development."

Sascha: "In the end it all comes down to meet us where we are. I am, as a customer, not able to understand everything the company does. They are the experts in the field. So in the end, I must be enabled to understand what they suggest. So I need to get the impression that they

> *can handle the technology, and they must be open to show me how it is done, that there is 'nothing to hide'."*

For concluding *openness,* it is found particularly pronounced in the database and emphasizes the importance of an open environment, the opening up by the provider himself as well as the willingness to enable the customer within the co-creation process for high-tech products.

4.2 Playfulness

Playfulness relates to customers' desire to play with different technologies, which does not necessarily correspond with the actual goal. Quite in contrast to the predominant credo in B2B research that business customers are unlikely to buy for emotional reasons (Eggert & Ulaga, 2002), the analysis revealed that there is a significant emotional value component. That component is referred to as *playfulness,* for which data suggest to hold true for a substantial part of the customers. Strongly marked by enjoyment within the co-creation process, it is the joy of experimentation and the willingness to indulge in trial and error. This value component is assigned to both the emotional and social dimension because the latter includes the exchange with other co-creating customers:

> *Sascha: "Sure, many of the engineers in our company want to have fun in such co-creation projects. It is particularly the exchange that we value with others. I know that this is in hard contrast to the picture of the 'rational buyer', but the reality is that we don't only chase the hard criteria."*

> *Andreas: "I'm the creative one who enjoys the process. I'm not talking about aesthetics, it's nerdy tech stuff. But also here you need creativity to combine different technologies sometimes. I usually consider it an experience with other creative guys with the same interests, and not 'only a job that pays my life'."*

Interestingly, several interviews underpin that customers have not always liked to participate in co-creation projects, but they were sent to such projects. Then, they have experienced *playfulness*, and have henceforth started to like participating in the co-creation of high-tech products:

> *Achim: "I haven't always liked coming to the company and spend time on long, intense development projects. But my manager insisted. Then, after several successful co-creation projects, I'm always looking forward to participate in such projects. To say it in a funny way, I'd say it's like a jam session for engineers."*

Looking at the approaches and structure of how that customers' desire for *playfulness* is satisfied by the provider, several interviews from different independent companies delineate a full day of intense co-creating, framed as an 'Innovation Day'[25]. Typically, as it is described by the interviewees, a company sets up such a day without setting clear goals. It is merely a rough idea that is communicated upfront which is then tackled with several engineers from various companies.

Shedding light on the 'Innovation Day' from the customer perspective, this approach is characterized by a trial-and-error experimentation. Often, objectives are not clearly set beforehand, but this is typically communicated by the provider in this way. Rather, creativity and an open environment are fostered in order to allow the customers to play with different possibilities. Interviewees find that quite promising and useful for perceiving *playfulness*. Products are not conceptualized on a theoretical or abstract level, concentrating on calculations or statistics, but rather on a practical level. After a brief meeting in a formal setting, participants move directly to the production and start testing. Here, the interviewed engineers stress explicitly that they have fun when it comes to the active, playful part:

[25] The 'Innovation Day' is also elaborated on from the provider's perspective in *Part II*. As some direct customers of the providers from the previous part were inquired, this approach equally appears in the analysis of the customer domain.

> *Jan: "One of the companies where I purchase does an 'Innovation Day' where they invite some customers. It's a pleasure to participate because it is so hands-on. We discuss a concept very briefly and go directly to the production and fiddle about different parameters."*

> *Anja: "I like these events because here I can play with the given variety and compose some different solutions. I do not necessarily that because it's in my job description, I do it just for fun."*

Looking at other approaches to satisfy customers' desire for *playfulness*, the data analysis delivers insights in manifold regards. For instance, the choice of the other co-creation participants from the other companies is one factor. Interviewees state that they need to be motivated, creative and willing to collaborate, too:

> *Tom: "I also like just playing with different possibilities. But only if we are at eye level with most of the participants, we can get in like a rush and test crazy stuff. It's somewhat of a collective creativity."*

The same holds true for participants by the providing company, who are supposed to conduct the overall co-creation process. But additionally, in favor to stimulate *playfulness,* the provider also takes the role of a moderator and challenges the participants. Participants are given demanding tasks, which evokes a competition among each other. Taking it with sporting ambition, most of the inquired customers state that they like perceiving competition in complex co-creation processes among the participants. Data suggest that this further motivates the participants to engage in the co-creation process:

> *Benno: "But for that [co-creating process], I expect to have some sparring partners in that interactive part who challenge the group, otherwise I need to fun myself. [...] When it's done well, there is a competition among us. I can demonstrate my expertise then, and who doesn't like showing what he can do?"*

The involvement of the appropriate stakeholder on a specialist level from the provider's side can also include other domains:

> *Friedrich: „I remember one time when I was invited to a company and they gave me the possibility to discuss a broad idea with an IT textile expert, spontaneously. We combined different solutions on the computer and explored totally new solutions. It was like playing with LEGO bricks – which was highly creative and inspiring. Based on that fuzzy design stuff, the company was able to develop new ideas later."*

As mentioned above, it is crucial to acknowledge that the value component *playfulness* does not apply to all business customers, as some come with a more efficiency-driven nature. In addition, neither do design-oriented customers always prefer such playful co-creation processes. This often depends on their current context and business situation:

> *Christian: "Yes, it's a joy to participate. But sure, it's not always this way. Sometimes I only need my tasks to be done, as quickly as possible."*

Summing up *playfulness,* the findings underpin the mandatory relation of *playfulness* to *openness,* because it becomes obvious that the customer is needed to be in the right mood so that he engages in co-creation. Although several studies stress the role of the co-creating company to conduct the process (Aarikka-Stenroos & Jaakkola, 2012; Piller et al., 2011), this study reveals manifold characteristics of the value component *playfulness* and delivers approaches how to address it in co-creation processes for high-tech products. In addition, for *playfulness,* it is argued that this component was underestimated in B2B research. However, this type of co-creation behavior is quite similar to the behavior of end customers who also value the process itself because of the feelings of enjoyment and creativity (e. g. Merle et al., 2010; Schreier, 2006). But as this study shows, the motivation is fundamentally different and the process comes with various requirements dissimilar to the consumer context. Furthermore, as business customers are involved to a high extent and as they heavily invest their time, the overall process comes with peculiarities in the B2B domain.

4.3 Self-fulfillment

Self-fulfillment describes customers' emotional satisfaction and pride in contributing to the development of a novel, high-tech product. Also, *self-fulfillment* refers to customers' perceived value of being part of a high-tech development. This is particularly striking as the business customer is typically not the user of the co-created offering (Vaquero Martín et al., 2016). It is classified as a purely emotional value component. Closely related to the aspect of competition (see *4.2 Playfulness*), customers describe *self-fulfillment* as one motivational factor in co-creating high-tech products:

> *Patrick: "It may sound stupid, but when you are involved in such an intense and innovative product development, you feel that it is also 'your' product. That is a factor that makes us motivated and proud."*

> *Kerstin: "Being in this high-tech industry that competes on a global level, pushing the technologies to the limit, belonging to the best experts in the field, that's why I'm so motivated in collaborative development projects. And I don't feel any competition between the participating companies, it's rather competing against our competitors overseas, there's a strong sense of belonging within the German textile industry."*

In addition, this showcases that the co-creation process itself is a source for creating value for the customer. And data suggest that this holds equally true for emotional value, not only functional components as related studies suggest (e. g. Aarikka-Stenroos & Jaakkola, 2012).

Diving deeper into the data, the following paragraphs describe how the value component *self-fulfillment* is triggered from the customer perspective, for which several approaches are exhibited. For instance, customers are given a prototype, a tangible outcome or, more abstract, a boundary object that they are later able to show and test in their own company. Often, this tangible outcome has been co-created during the 'Innovation Day':

> *Carl: "The last time, I even got a prototype at the end of the day that I could present to my colleagues the next day. I was surprised myself, but that was a great experience."*

Another approach concerns a careful handling of the contribution of the participating customer. Interviewees state that it is important for them to recognize their contribution to the co-created high-tech product. Customers are keen to understand their own contribution. Especially in high-tech product co-creation, this is vital, because many stakeholders are involved, which hinders a selective demarcation of single contributions. The engineers inquired specify that even if it is only details they contributed, it is important for them to recognize that to perceive *self-fulfillment*:

> *Bert: "It is important that I know what my contribution was – otherwise I might get the feeling that I did not really contribute something to it."*

> *Benno: "There are always many parties and departments involved in these co-creation projects. You lose the overview very quickly. I find it very important that the company keeps track and demonstrates later who contributed which idea, who has had the best ideas and so on... I want to see what I achieved."*

In this vein, the interviewees describe this topic as a particularly important aspect that creates value in their domain, because they perceive that they often cannot identify their individual contribution. This is especially the case in rather complex, joint development projects. This is considered as a facet of *self-fulfillment* because it relates to the emotional satisfaction of participating and contributing to such projects:

> *Tom: "Having a direct influence on the product... that's what we all dream of or not? I mean, not seeing the impact of your work is one of the issues nowadays: you work a lot on a project and don't see any result afterwards."*

> *Gregor: "You know, there are only few experts worldwide in specialized, complex geotextiles. And coming together, working on the next gen[eration] products and see my direct impact, that's a highlight for me. You feel like a chosen as there are only few guys who could do the job."*

Overall, similar indications for *self-fulfillment* are described in the consumer context (Franke, Schreier, & Kaiser, 2010; Schreier, 2006), but with one crucial distinction: while consumers typically keep and use the product themselves, business customers rather buy on behalf of their company in their role as purchasers. They do not use it themselves usually (Vaquero Martín et al., 2016). Therefore, it is argued that the value component *self-fulfillment* comes with peculiarities for the B2B context and sheds light on the motivation of the interviewees which is not rational.

5 Conclusions

The overall goal of *Part III* was to explore customers' value in high-tech product co-creation. For the functional side of value, a rather rich picture was drawn from the literature. Then, a shortcoming in extant research was shown in the area of emotional and social value components in B2B co-creation. This shortcoming was targeted with an explorative interview study that focused on the customer perspective. In total, 42 interviews were conducted in the German textile industry with customers that come with an engineering background, as this domain is typically concerned with co-creating high-tech products. The exploratory analysis focused on neglected areas of emotional and social value components and revealed three novel value components, namely *openness, playfulness* and *self-fulfillment.* It is argued that these findings comprise empirical evidence that business customers value emotional and social value in co-creation processes, which has been widely neglected in extant B2B research.

Although this study is embedded in the dissertation at hand, it comprises an individual theoretical contribution, managerial implications and limitations. The following *sections* illuminate these areas.

5.1 Contribution to research

This study brings the customer perspective on value components in the co-creation process for high-tech products into sharper focus. It puts special emphasis on the neglected areas of emotional and social value (Arslanagic-Kalajdzic & Zabkar, 2017; Prior, 2013). It is argued for a contribution to research in at least three regards.

First, the better understanding of the emotional and social value components allows for better conceptualizing the engagement of business customers into problem-solving activities (Nickerson & Zenger, 2004). As a result, it also advances the works around eliciting sticky information (von Hippel, 1994), which is one major challenge regarding the co-creation of high-tech products (La Rocca et al., 2016; Nordin & Kowalkowski, 2010). Further, exploring the neglected areas of emotional and social value in B2B, this study makes a strong contribution against the picture of the rational, purely functionally-driven business customer. Because so far, the typical description of business customers has been fundamentally different: they are said to source strategically and to buy for economic, not emotional reasons (Eggert & Ulaga, 2002).

Second, the identified emotional and social value components add a better understanding on how successful co-creation is designed along different customers' preferences (Frow et al., 2015; Malshe & Friend, 2018). This insight is offered from the customer perspective, which has been under researched especially in the B2B area (Arslanagic-Kalajdzic & Zabkar, 2017; Mustak et al., 2013; Prior, 2013).

Third, related studies are especially based in the B2C context, for instance in the research strand of mass customization. It holds several promising indications regarding the precise design of a co-creation process. For instance, Merle et al. (2010) found creativity and enjoyment during the co-creation process for the consumer context. Another study by Franke et al. (2010) emphasizes the emotional satisfaction by contributing to a unique product design. As a result, this study expanded the understanding of such emotional and social value for the B2B context. With that, the conceptualization of value can be advanced also for the B2B domain (Candi & Kahn, 2016; Füller et al., 2011). This study adds one puzzle piece in the pursuit to catching up with B2C research.

In conclusion, this study extends knowledge on customer value of co-creating high-tech products for business customers. To some extent, it explains business customer behavior on the individual level. It also provides explanations, why certain value components play a role in the B2B context and how they are captured from a customer perspective. Also, it follows the call for multi-dimensional conceptualization of value in B2B by Candi and Kahn (2016) by suggesting three value components *openness, playfulness* and *self-fulfillment* on the dimensions of emotional and social value.

As clearly stated in the findings section, it is decisive to acknowledge that the described emotional and social components do not apply to all business customers, as some are characterized by a more efficiency-driven behavior. Moreover, in some cases, depending on the current business situation, neither do design-oriented customers always desire *playfulness* and *self-fulfillment*.

5.2 Managerial implications

The most immediate managerial implication emerges from the existence of the identified value components *playfulness* and *self-fulfillment*, especially with regard to redesigning novel co-creation processes. For instance, it appears obvious to decrease direct interaction with efficiency-driven customers. They particularly value functional value, which is best captured with rational arguments. Moreover, iterations of design steps increase the effort on the customer side which is eventually not wanted by this type. For the design-oriented type, it is the opposite: increasing creative collaboration and creating an according atmosphere provides value. As the database suggests, the organization of an 'Innovation Day' is fruitful, if properly conducted. As a consequence, maintaining the high degree of face-to-face for the design-oriented type seems to be a reasonable avenue for mastering the stretch between the desire to experience *playfulness* and *self-fulfillment* in intense co-creation and valuable process outcomes. Raising the question how to identify whether a customer is design-oriented or efficiency-driven, it is reasonable to directly ask them in an early stage, as the database suggests. This is feasible, because typically, customers are well-placed to articulate their basic preferences in this regard. Consequently, the findings of this research particularly help providing companies to better design the process along customers' preferences. This allows the provider to better engage the customer into co-creation (Frow et al., 2015; Mustak et al., 2013).

Furthermore, the findings of *Part III* inform the deployment of a toolkit. While the idea of a toolkit to replace (parts of) the co-creation process has been successfully implemented in B2C markets for many years (Franke & Piller, 2003), it can be expected that these findings cannot be simply copied to B2B markets. In this context, Fauska et al. (2014) found that high-tech products present specific features which cannot be easily described on an online sales platform. In line with that, the findings strongly suggest that a part of the process must take place offline due to the high complexity. However, a partial standardization of the process seems attractive especially in light of the efficiency-driven customer: a very simple approach is to separate rather uncomplex from complex tasks to increase efficiency, for instance using checklists or a toolkit to capture some information. Inter alia, the following *part* is dedicated to that task.

5.3 Limitations and further research

The sample offers a rather big database with its 42 interviews, but it is still limited to the high-tech textile industry in Germany. Given this, using and enhancing the findings beyond the current empirical setting is advised. Regarding peculiarities of this study's setting, the high-tech textile industry typically faces the challenge of dealing with the complexities of intangible product characteristics such as specific functions and haptics, which usually means that the customer needs to have the product in his hand to assess its quality. Nonetheless, limitations of such kind can be found in other industries, too, wherever multi-sensory experiences are central. In other terms, they are synonymous for many other facets that are difficult to articulate.

Another limitation is that this is still an early exploration of emotional and social components in B2B co-creation processes. While the study adds insights to this field and provides deep insight in current customer perceived value, the findings remain descriptive. An evaluation ideally chooses a quantitative approach for testing the relevance of the identified value components also for other business customers.

Part IV – Designing a toolkit for the co-creation of high-tech products

L. K. Grafmüller, *Co-Creation of High-Tech Products in the B2B Domain*,
Markt- und Unternehmensentwicklung Markets and Organisations,
https://doi.org/10.1007/978-3-658-28412-1_4

1 Needs and objectives[26]

> *"Using direct customer contacts for innovations and continuous improving of the processes [is irrevocable], customers can never be fully switched to [online]."* (Fauska et al., 2014, p. 20)

Part IV picks up the third research gap (see *Chapter 2* of *Part I*) and points out opportunities for the usage of toolkits in the context of high-tech product co-creation. It builds an artefact for a real-life setting, using design science research (DSR), and includes both the provider and customer perspective. *Part IV* is embedded in the dissertation as illustrated in *Figure 16*:

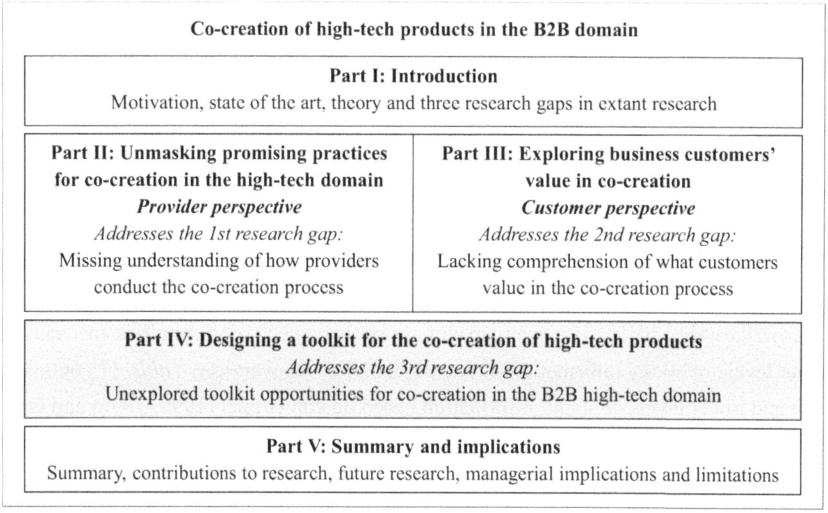

Figure 16: Embedding of *Part IV* in the dissertation

[26] An earlier version of this study has been presented at *The 2017 World Mass Customization & Personalization Conference*, Aachen, Germany. Further, an updated version has been presented at the *8th International Conference on Mass Customization and Personalization in Central Europe,* Novi Sad, Serbia. All publications of the author are listed in Annex I.

The following paragraphs depict the need for this study and derive the research question to tackle the third research gap.

High-tech products are typically co-created in personal and time-consuming interactions as they require intense explanation by experts at the provider side (Davies et al., 2007; Gosling & Naim, 2009; La Rocca et al., 2016). Here, interaction and information costs between customers and providers are high (Madhavaram & Appan, 2010). Research suggests that such offerings are co-created most smoothly in face-to-face settings (Aarikka-Stenroos & Jaakkola, 2012; Anderson, 1996; Fauska et al., 2014; Haas et al., 2012; Heide & John, 1990; Hemetsberger & Godula, 2007; La Rocca et al., 2016; Lynch & Chernatony, 2007; Vaquero Martín et al., 2016). In this context, the problem-solving perspective explains that high levels of sticky information are best faced in personal interactions between customer and provider (von Hippel, 1990b, 1994). This is also supported by the media richness theory explaining that high media richness, i. e. face-to-face settings, is best to address high information complexity in interactions (Daft & Lengel, 1986; Dennis & Valacich, 1999).

This need for face-to-face explicates why toolkits are usually rather not used in the context of high-tech products (e. g. Fauska et al., 2014; Laage-Hellman et al., 2014), as they have a limited suitability for facing these particularly high levels of sticky information (von Hippel, 1994). This is especially pronounced when dealing with rather complex offerings (Aarikka-Stenroos & Jaakkola, 2012; La Rocca et al., 2016; Nordin & Kowalkowski, 2010). However, extant research neglects opportunities to capture lower levels of sticky information in this domain. For an overview, *Table 11* contrasts high and lower levels of sticky information based on von Hippel (1990, 1994) and Ogawa (1998).

Lower levels of sticky information are typically also part of the required information (von Hippel, 1990b), and capturing them with a toolkit seems to make sense to lower information costs. To put it clearly, the customer could easily provide this information alone by using a toolkit (von Hippel, 1990a, 1994), as he is guided toward providing the required information (von Hippel, 2001). Following the principles of task partitioning, this would not be done in a customer-provider interaction anymore, but the customer would do it by himself (von Hippel, 1990a).

Table 11: Higher and lower levels of sticky information[27]

	High levels of sticky information	Lower levels of sticky information
Description	High information stickiness entails that it is difficult to transfer from one locus to another, because it cannot be verbalized and is often embodied in a certain context (Ogawa, 1998; von Hippel, 1994).	It is less costly to transfer information on lower levels of stickiness (Ogawa, 1998; von Hippel, 1994), because such information is less complex, and one can diffuse it in a simpler way (von Hippel, 1990b).
Elicitation mode	High levels of sticky information are best transferred in a synchronous way, i. e. by using close interactions and face-to-face (von Hippel, 1994).	Lower levels of sticky information can be captured asynchronously (Ogawa, 1998).
Example	*"Suppose that one cannot replicate and diffuse the information related to "how to run an automobile assembly plant efficiently" without replicating the embodiment of that information - the plant operating team and perhaps the plant itself."* (von Hippel, 1990b, p. 4)	It is easier *"to replicate and diffuse the information embodied in a catalyst or computer chip by making and selling copies of those products."* (von Hippel, 1990b, p. 5)

This study focuses on understanding how lower levels of sticky information are captured with a toolkit to better prepare the subsequent face-to-face interaction. This is illustrated in the right column of *Table 11*. Toolkits are acknowledged for reducing interaction and information costs between customers and providers (Franke & Piller, 2003; von Hippel, 2001; von Hippel & Katz, 2002). Using a toolkit to capture lower levels of sticky information appears especially promising in the context of high-tech product co-creation to reduce the significant information costs (La Rocca et al., 2016; Madhavaram & Appan, 2010; Olausson & Berggren, 2010).

Although such toolkit approaches seem promising, related research on toolkit designs in domains with high product complexity is scant. Since the co-creation of high-tech products requires deep knowledge on the final use, several fields of expertise for their development and a wide breadth of knowledge and skills, co-creation processes in this domain are challenging. Moreover, the introduction of information systems comes with

[27] Both von Hippel (1990b) and Ogawa (1998) argue for different levels of stickiness. While von Hippel (1990b) distinguishes mainly between *"sticky"* and *"non-sticky"* (ibid., p. 5) in his early work, Ogawa (1998) elaborates on different degrees inbetween, stretching a spectrum from lower to higher levels of stickiness. The research at hand follows the latter understanding, the spectrum, and assumes that the toolkit's task ranges in the lower to medium range of stickiness, as its goal is to guide the customer toward providing desired requirements.

numerous pitfalls especially regarding complex offerings (Fauska et al., 2014; Laage-Hellman et al., 2014).

Several B2B companies have already experimented with information systems for reducing information costs, mainly with configurators, which prerequisite a predefined solution space (Haug et al., 2009). Other approaches deal with partial configurability (Forza & Salvador, 2007, p. 30). However, it does not solve the problem when dealing with an ETO context, i. e., a part of the offering is developed exclusively for one customer (Gosling & Naim, 2009; Haug et al., 2013). These domains exhibit undefined solution spaces, which widely excludes traditional configurator approaches that allow for configuring and directly purchase the product after (Gilmore & Pine, 1997). Also, other toolkit approaches known from the consumer domain seem inappropriate, as they allow the customer to discover his preferences in creative trial-and-error processes with a major emphasis on visual attributes (Franke & Piller, 2004; Thomke & von Hippel, 2002)[28].

Having set the emphasis on lower levels of sticky information, one has to ask what kind of such information is helpful for the provider to better prepare the co-creation process in this context. Further, capturing it with a toolkit must be examined. Tackling the third research gap to point out opportunities for toolkit usage, the research question reads as follows:

> *RQ to address the third research gap:*
> *What information on lower levels of stickiness is helpful for the provider and how can it be captured with a toolkit?*

For answering this question, *Part IV* builds an artefact using DSR (Hevner, March, Park, & Ram, 2004; Peffers & Tuunanen, 2007). This approach provides a clear structure of designing, demonstrating and evaluating the artefact. Furthermore, it is particularly helpful due to its iterative, multi-cyclic adaptation of the toolkit while based in a real-

[28] Reichwald and Piller (2009) provide an overview on toolkits (ibid., p. 189-197). The focus is mainly on the consumer domain. The authors expose several examples for *toolkits for user innovation*, following von Hippel (2001), that allow the customer to create virtual prototypes (Reichwald & Piller, 2009).

life setting. Since this approach comes with a high degree of novelty in the B2B high-tech domain, this study uses a qualitative research design to explore all its peculiarities in the given context (Eisenhardt, 1989).

The study was carried out in cooperation with B2B companies in the German high-tech textile industry. The development of the artefact is informed by five focus groups with 20 participants in total. From the companies, both customers' and providers' insights were covered, involving procurement and sales managers from the companies. The artefact is a use case diagram which highlights four identified functions. For instance, the function *specifying the final use of the product* is crucial, as the provider is enabled to better understand the customer's context based on that information. Another function narrows down customers' requirements which allow the provider to conclude several properties of the textile. Both serve to better prepare the face-to-face interaction and to save costs. Then, for one of the companies, an artefact-based toolkit is built using the company's specific product portfolio specifications and decision tree. Developing an instance for a specific case allows gathering precise feedback by the participants because the toolkit shows real-life examples without abstraction (Hevner et al., 2004, 2004). The evaluation part, conducted in the focal company, is informed by seven in-depth interviews to help describe how the toolkit helps reduce information costs. Findings describe how the toolkit supports the overall process and what functions help in particular. Contribution to research relates to calls for more research on tools that enable effective co-creation (Barczak, 2012; Frow et al., 2015). The conclusion derives a discussion and managerial implications also for related industries that deal with high complexity and clarify what toolkit functions are likely to be translatable.

This empirical study encompasses seven *chapters* in line with the DSR approach (Hevner et al., 2004). *Chapter 2* starts off with the theoretical underpinning and the problem definition. *Chapter 3* focuses on the research design by detailing the steps of the DSR, sampling, data collection, and data analysis. *Chapter 4* designs and develops the artefact. *Chapter 5* demonstrates the artefact-based toolkit that is subsequently evaluated in *Chapter 6*. Eventually, *Chapter 7* completes this part with the conclusions.

2 Theoretical underpinning

This *chapter* introduces the theoretical underpinning for this DSR-oriented study. It provides an overview of the relevant topics, namely media richness in high-tech product co-creation and the research on toolkits. Eventually, the last *section* concludes with the problem definition.

2.1 Media richness and the co-creation of high-tech products

Often, the co-creation of high-tech products is associated with challenges such as the lack of efficiency or efficacy (see *Part I, Chapter 2*). Especially, high-tech products need heavy explanation due to their intangible features and many, time-consuming interactions (Davies et al., 2007; Gosling & Naim, 2009; La Rocca et al., 2016). Research has reached consensus that such offerings are co-created most smoothly in face-to-face settings (Aarikka-Stenroos & Jaakkola, 2012; Anderson, 1996; Fauska et al., 2014; Haas et al., 2012; Heide & John, 1990; Hemetsberger & Godula, 2007; La Rocca et al., 2016; Lynch & Chernatony, 2007; Vaquero Martín et al., 2016).

One explanation for this need for face-to-face is delivered by the media richness theory, introduced by Daft and Lengel (1986) and refined by Dennis and Valacich (1999). Used also in other recent studies on co-creation (e. g. Mahr et al., 2014), this theory distinguishes different media along their dimension of richness and explains different media choices. Poor media such as mail are used for simple, structured communication tasks, and rich media are used when uncertainty and equivocality are high, and when information stickiness is high (von Hippel, 1994). Daft and Lengel (1986) develop a model illustrating the task complexity and media richness, including also an ideal band with the corresponding effective media use. Outside of the band, the chosen media is either over-complicating or over-simplifying the task. *Figure 17* illustrates the media richness theory based on a two-dimension matrix by Reichwald, Möslein, Sachenbacher, Englberger, and Oldenburg (1998).

Looking through the lens of media richness theory, it is argued that extant studies focus on how very high levels of sticky information are elicited in product development (Aarikka-Stenroos & Jaakkola, 2012; Anderson, 1996; Fauska et al., 2014; Haas et al., 2012; Heide & John, 1990; La Rocca et al., 2016; Lynch & Chernatony, 2007; Vaquero Martín et al., 2016). But they neglect how the specifications with lower levels of stickiness, that are typically also part of the process, are captured. In *Figure 17,* this shortcoming in the literature ranges in the lower to medium area in the two-dimension matrix. These two areas are marked with stars in *Figure 17*, based on Reichwald et al. (1998, p. 57):

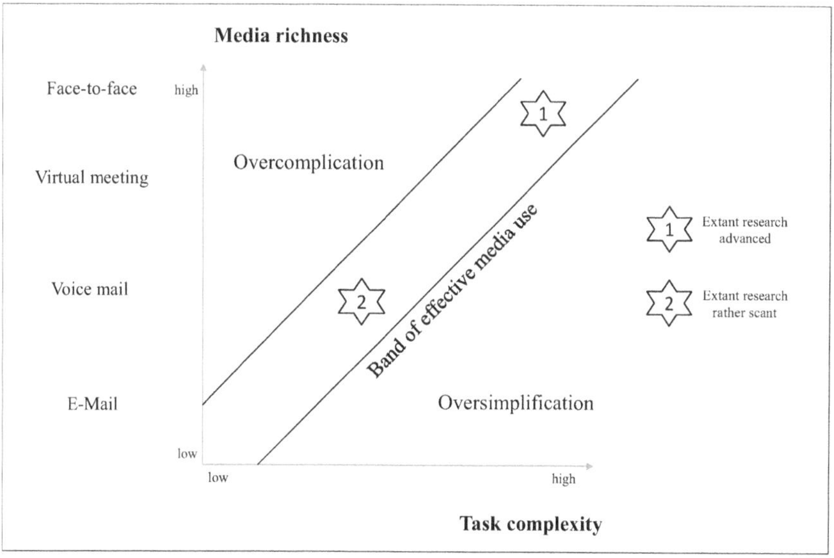

Figure 17: Media richness theory and high-tech product co-creation research[29]

Before diving deeper, one objection may arise concerning the justification of this study: it is reasonable to ask for the actual need to focus on less sticky specifications captured by a toolkit. This objection may seem justified because in extant research, for instance in the area of mass customization, numerous studies deal with that topic of capturing

[29] Two-dimension matrix for the media richness theory derived from Reichwald et al. (1998, p. 57), based on Daft and Lengel (1986) and Rice (1992).

rather simple specifications with a toolkit (e. g. Fogliatto, Da Silveira, & Borenstein, 2012; Piller, Schubert, Koch, & Möslein, 2005). In this context, it is argued for two major differences for the present study.

First, current research does not address the question what information is both on lower levels of stickiness and at the same time helpful for the provider in high-tech product co-creation. Second, extant research stresses difficulties in early phases in co-creating complex offerings. Finding a starting point to co-create is found quite problematic. For instance, Aarikka-Stenroos and Jaakkola (2012) unveiled that, especially at the beginning, it is difficult to focus the face-to-face interaction on issues that really need rich media. They found that many details hinder dealing with the actual elicitation of high levels of sticky information. They further state that *"suppliers felt that it is impossible even to start the process without information on the customer's needs, budget, schedule, usage, and business context"* (ibid., p. 20). They consider such information a critical resource to start off. The authors also found that asking for the actual, underlying goal is useful, instead of rather technical product specifications in co-creation. Such information appears to be on lower levels of stickiness as the customer typically knows the eventual goal, for instance. As this requires a lower level of media richness, a toolkit is capable to master the task and to deliver valuable information to the provider.

The primary goal of this study is to facilitate the joint problem solving process between customer and provider with helpful information that is gathered with the toolkit. This facilitation is achieved by capturing relevant information with the toolkit, and then focusing the joint problem solving on the elicitation of high levels of sticky information (von Hippel, 1994). With that, the provider is enabled to better prepare the problem-solving activities, which enhances efficiency and efficacy (Nickerson & Zenger, 2004).

2.2 Toolkits for co-creating high-tech products

While sales processes have been mainly carried out in face-to-face settings (Anderson, 1996; Lynch & Chernatony, 2007), they are getting more and more digitized (Nambisan, Lyytinen, Majchrzak, & Song, 2017). This digitalization trend has also been noticed in B2B settings (Zahay, Schultz, & Kumar, 2015). This implies that the interaction between customer and provider changes (Miller, 2012). For instance, B2B portals assist employees and clients to have better decision-making capabilities through access to aggregated information (Clarke & Flaherty, 2003). Another early study deals with a choice menu with various features and options for configuring product specifications, which is found helpful in the early stage of customer involvement (Liechty, Ramaswamy, & Cohen, 2001; Slywotzky, 2000).

Toolkits in this study aim to capture customer information with lower levels of stickiness in an efficient way, which allows for postponing the highly sticky specification part to the upcoming face-to-face co-creation process. This also allows for task partitioning as the customer is in charge of providing the initial requirements by means of the toolkit by himself (von Hippel, 1990a).

Toolkits reduce interaction and information costs between customers and providers (von Hippel, 2001; von Hippel & Katz, 2002). Therefore, toolkits are categorized as systems, which are provided by the company to their customers. They permit transferring customers' need information to the provider and vice-versa transferring solution information. This study focuses on toolkits that specify customers' requirements (e. g. Naik, 2017, p. 4).

Summing it up, a reduction of interaction and information costs is targeted by separating lower levels from the high levels of stickiness. In the current transition from innovation to digital innovation (Nambisan et al., 2017), this study focuses on the early phase of a co-creation process by capturing less sticky information with a toolkit. Also, it tackles the problem described by Aarikka-Stenroos and Jaakkola (2012) that providers struggle to even start the process without basic customer information. A toolkit captures this kind of information and allows informing this process upfront.

2.3 Problem definition

The need for this study is presented along a twofold problem definition. They are illustrated in *Figure 18* and deeper depicted afterwards. Overall, it is argued that there is both a research gap and a motivation derived from extant research to address lower levels of sticky information with a toolkit.

1st problem:	**2nd problem:**
Efficiency and efficacy are often lacking in the co-creation of high-tech products as interaction and information costs are high.	Providers struggle to start off the process to co-create high-tech products, because they lack information to prepare the co-creation process.

Figure 18: Twofold problem definition of *Part IV*

The first problem is that the interaction and information costs between customers and providers are high (Madhavaram & Appan, 2010), which hinders efficient co-creation. For capturing customers' requirements, providers currently use face-to-face. Approaches to lower interaction and information costs, using IT, have not been exploited in the domain of co-creating high-tech products.

The second problem is that the provider often lacks information in order to start off the co-creation process. This is why providers struggle to find a starting point (Aarikka-Stenroos & Jaakkola, 2012). Consequently, starting into the co-creation process in a more informed way appears fruitful, but this is an unsolved problem. Using a toolkit with that aim is highly promising to streamline the overall process.

3 Method and data

The method and data *section* commences with the DSR research approach used in this study to build the artefact in a real-life setting. Then, the data as well as the data analysis are set out.

3.1 Research approach

This research aims at answering the question what information is on lower levels of stickiness and at the same time helpful for the provider. Further, it responds to the question how this information can be captured with a toolkit. This is depicted in *Chapters 4, 5* and *6* in this *part.* It focuses on a problem in real-life and builds an artefact that delivers concrete solutions to this task. With that goal, the DSR approach by Peffers and Tuunanen (2007) appears suitable. The DSR approach provides a clear structure of designing, demonstrating and evaluating the artefact. Further, the iterative, multi-cyclic adaptation of the artefact is helpful to improve it informed by real life. *Figure 19* illustrates the DSR approach for this study.

Since extant research has not dealt with such toolkit approaches (e. g. Fauska et al., 2014; Laage-Hellman et al., 2014), this research is characterized by a qualitative research design. This is particularly useful for deep descriptions in the context and to uncover underlying lines of thought (Eisenhardt, 1989). Particularly, the study is designed to explain the different facets of the artefact from the perspective of the interviewees. In this vein, Tidd and Bessant (2013) argue for its usefulness as this allows for being also valuable to other contexts in innovation research (Tidd & Bessant, 2018).

For the artefact development and evaluation, focus groups and in-depth interviews are used. From the companies, customers and providers are involved, i. e. also procurement and sales managers.

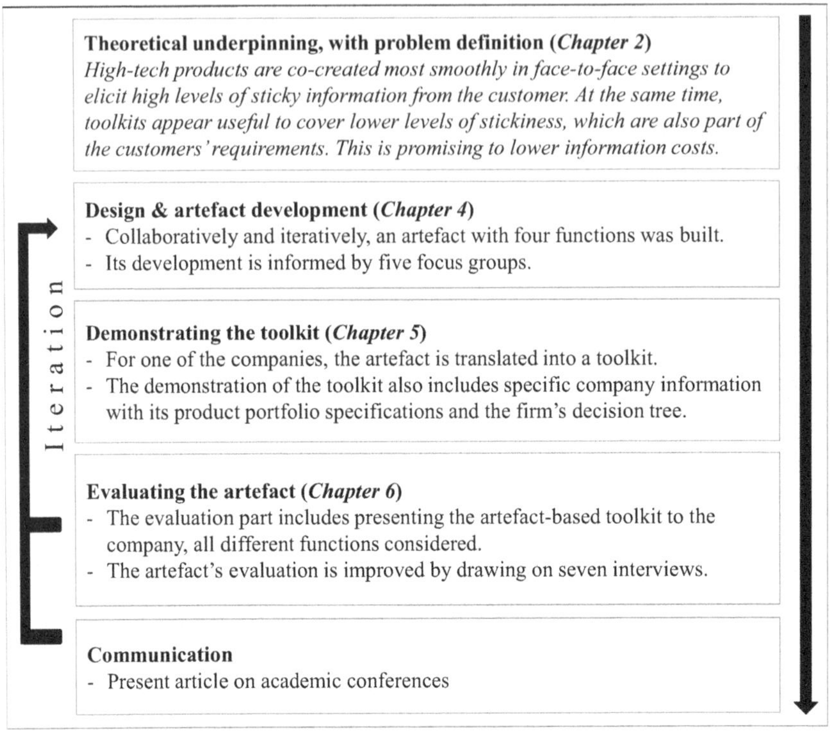

Figure 19: DSR approach of *Part IV* by Peffers and Tuunanen (2007)

3.2 Sample and data

The artefact developed in this study is based on the interactions with B2B companies from the German high-tech textile industry[30]. For setting up the artefact, five focus groups were conducted. Each focus group represents one joint effort to solve the problems described above. All companies deal with high product complexity. Already nowadays, this branch heavily co-creates custom products, but does not exploit toolkit opportunities. It is argued that this domain is likely to benefit from a toolkit such as described in this study. Companies subject of this study are characterized by three commonalities.

[30] A description of the context of this research with examples is provided in *Part I, Chapter 3.*

First, high complexity is typically faced with one-to-one marketing. Intense customer-provider interactions serve to co-create the offering. Second, they provide mainly high-tech offerings for industrial customers, for which at least one part is co-created. Thirdly, there are no supporting toolkits in the process. The data for this study was gathered in these companies, for which additional information is provided in *Table 12*. For the sampling of study participants in the interviews and focus groups, sales managers, technical directors, procurement managers etc. were chosen (see *Table 12*). The provider's and the customer's view are covered, nonetheless from the same companies. Following a purposeful sampling approach (Patton, 1990), experienced stakeholders were chosen (more than ten years working experience in this domain). The focus groups involved 20 participants in total; and seven in-depth interviews were conducted in the focal firm.

Table 12: Overview of companies and focus group data for *Part IV*

Brief company description	Number of participants	Position of interviewee	Staff	Focus group length
The first company, where two focus groups were conducted, is the focal company for which the demonstrator was set up to evaluate the artefact.				
Manufacturer of coated fabrics with specific functions, e. g., tear-proof, heat-resistant, cold-resistant, emboss-ment	5 participants	CEO, Head of Sales, Procurement Manager, Sales Managers	250	122 min
	3 participants	Technical Director, Procurement Manager, Sales Manager		115 min
High-quality fabric manufacturer with specific functions for indoor use, e. g., acoustic insulating and fireproof	4 participants	CEO, Technical Director, Procure-ment Manager	50	138 min
Manufacturer of yarn for technical textiles with specific functions, e. g., tensile strength, heat- & cold-resistant	4 participants	CEO, Sr. Development Manager, Sales Manager	100	161 min
Service provider for technical textiles, adding specific functions, e. g., water-resistant, fireproof	4 participants	CEO, Chief Developer, Sales Manager, Procurement Manager	100	122 min

The data contain two parts: focus groups to set up the artefact and interviews for evaluating. The first part is represented by five focus groups in different textile companies. Focus groups are particularly helpful to foster dynamic discussions among the participants, allowing for group interaction (Kitzinger, 1995). For this study's purposes, this appeared suitable because it was attempted to elicit innovative approaches for exploiting IT opportunities in co-creation. Three to five participants were involved, in line with recommended practice (Morgan, 1997, p. 43). It took place as follows.

After a brief motivation of the topic, participants were supposed to discuss a series of open questions derived from the problem definition (see *2.3. Problem definition* and *Table 13*). The questions and tasks for the focus groups overlap to a certain extent, which served to approach the topic from different starting points and to gather multi-faceted insight. It was done with four blocks:

Table 13: Task description and open questions for focus group participants of *Part IV*

The open questions with their introduction were read by the moderating researcher to the focus group participants. Afterwards, focus group participants were supposed to discuss the topic, to reach a shared understanding and finally to compile solution approaches.
1. Often, the co-creation process is difficult to start off, because some basic information of the customer and his context is missing. This entails that the process is inefficient and characterized by trial-and-error. What information would help you to start off the process? At the same time, can customers easily give that information without deeper explanation (e. g. via mail/drop-down menu)? (Aarikka-Stenroos & Jaakkola, 2012; Laage-Hellman et al., 2014)
2. Face-to-face is especially powerful for the elicitation of complex requirements. This is the major reason why you prefer to meet up in person to discuss the complex issues. But typically, there are also uncomplex specifications besides the complex ones that you try to gather. Please elaborate on these uncomplex specifications! What are they? What is their importance?
3. We know from your industry that toolkits such as configurators are rather not used[31]. What are the reasons for that? What are shortcomings and barriers of configurators for your industry?
4. [Based on results from the previous question,] turning the perspective, what are drivers for a toolkit for your industry? What functions need to be included? What specifications can be entered by the customer? What specifications are, at the same time, articulable by the customer and helpful for you?
The moderating researcher only intervened when focus group participants lost their focus on the question, or when deeper descriptions were desired at some point. In the latter case, queries aimed at getting deeper insight and better descriptions.

All focus groups were recorded and transcribed. In a final presentation, where every company was present, a first version of the artefact with its functions was presented to mirror the objectives derived from the focus groups. With a slightly improved version, the artefact was used to set up a toolkit for one of the participating companies. This allowed building the toolkit for this company's specific product portfolio and internal decision tree. Utilizing data from the focal company is useful in order to gather unfiltered feedback as interviewees are able to directly relate the content to their firm. By

[31] Within a project of the research initiative *futureTEX* (funded by the BMBF, FKZ: 03ZZ0604A), a survey of 68 textile companies from the German textile industry revealed that very few firms have experimented with configurators (or toolkits in general). Data are based on http://clicresearch.org/basisvorhaben-mc/wp-content/uploads/sites/17/2015/09/Abschlussdokument_Basisvorhaben_MassCustomization.pdf, retrieved October 2nd 2018.

doing so, it was sought to reduce abstraction which is helpful in search of greater relevance due to the use of unfiltered and real rather than artificial contexts (Harrison & List, 2004; Hevner et al., 2004).

Following DSR, the evaluation was done by using the second part of the data. The iterative evaluation process was informed by seven interviews conducted in the focal company. Here, interviewees were presented the artefact-based toolkit presented in *Chapter 5,* and they were supposed to elaborate freely on each function and overall impressions. The selection of both the focus group participants as well as the interviewees included the Technical Director, Head of Sales, Procurement Manager and Sales Managers. Each of the seven interviews took one hour approximately, being a total of 434 min of interview data. All interviewees are considered experienced to assess the toolkit whether it really facilitates their daily work in direct comparison. Also here, both perspectives of customer and provider have been taken into account, nonetheless from only one company in the evaluation part. The artefact and toolkit were iteratively improved and extended by constantly integrating the feedback (Verschuren & Hartog, 2005). Interviewees were also supposed to elaborate on their impressions with notes afterwards, and then their additional feedback was collected in short follow-up interviews. All data for this study was recorded and transcribed.

3.3 Data analysis

Since extant research has not dealt with such approaches as described in this study, it makes sense to approach the topic in an explorative way. A qualitative method is especially recommended when developed concepts need to be deeply described within their context (Eisenhardt, 1989). Following DSR, the analysis was characterized by iteratively improving the artifact based on data from focus groups as well as semi-structured face-to-face interviews that followed the demonstration of the toolkit.

For both focus groups and interviews, a qualitative data analysis was based on the coding procedure suggested by Corbin and Strauss (2008), deviating mainly regarding the underlying goal. More precisely, the focus group analysis targeted the artefact development for uncovering and describing the functions, while the interviews served to understand how the toolkit serves to ease co-creation processes with high-tech products. Multiple phenomena were assumed to explore, which is why data analysis was organized in a flexible and constantly comparative way (Glaser, 1965). Overall, the focus of this analysis was put on capturing lower levels of sticky information. Some features that were also considered useful were excluded, such as flawless repurchase etc., since they are not related to co-creation activities.

For analyzing the data of the focus groups, the coding procedure by Corbin and Strauss (2008) was utilized. With the goals of this study and problems defined (see *2.3 Problem definition*), initial codes were defined by the researcher. Then, the code list was expanded and targeted the functions of the artefact, condensing the data by constantly comparing and iterating the focus group data with extant research (Glaser, 1965; Miles et al., 2014). Both induction and deduction were combined in this qualitative research for the artefact development (Glaser, 1965). The data analysis of the one-on-one interviews for the evaluation part followed the same procedure on a theoretical level, but the goal was different: emphasis was put on unmasking and understanding the benefits and pitfalls of the artefact-based toolkit. It was touched upon the four functions of the artefact to set up the initial codes that were revised and expanded afterwards. For improving, preliminary results were outlined in short follow-up interviews via telephone, that were conducted a couple of weeks after the personal interviews. Feedback was fed back into the artefact and toolkit development.

4 Design & artefact development

This study aims to capture lower levels of sticky information with a toolkit in order to better prepare the subsequent face-to-face interaction. In this *chapter*, an artefact for that purpose is set up following the DSR approach.

For the artefact development, data from five focus groups were examined. Various functions and requirements were identified. The artefact is a use case diagram: a use case diagram is a tool for illustrating the functional requirements of a system that allows the inclusion of various stakeholders (Shen & Liu, 2003). In this study, it serves to illustrate both sides and links the examined functions with both parties that are involved in the co-creation process. The use case diagram in *Figure 20* highlights the four functions identified, that are afterwards deeper depicted in *Table 14*. It is also elaborated on the order to structure the four functions. A closer description with underpinning data derived from the focus groups follows. While the artefact mainly helps the provider to reduce information costs, there are also benefits for the customer.

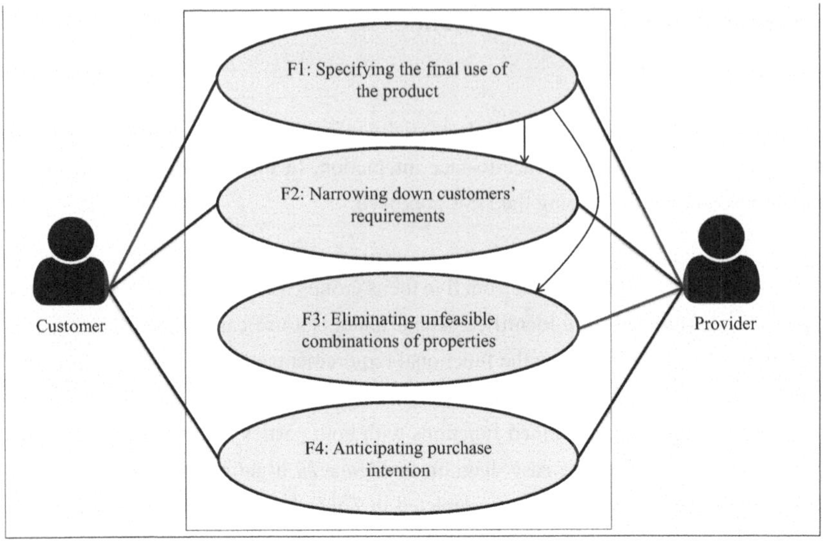

Figure 20: Use case diagram of the artefact[32]

The four functions (F1 – F4) presented in the use case diagram in *Figure 20* are depicted with an example in *Table 14.* The connections from 'customer' and 'provider' linked to the individual functions showcase the access by the stakeholders. To give an example, the customer does not have access to F3. Furthermore, the arrows in the use case diagram underpin that information collected with that function has an impact on another function. For instance, information gathered by F1 eliminates certain combinations of textile properties targeted with F3.

[32] In the use case diagram, secondary functions such as *Create customer account* or *Login to customer account*, are excluded for better clarity and mere focus on this study's goal.

Table 14: Function description of the artefact

Function	Description	Example
F1: Specifying the final use of the product	This function allows the provider to understand for what the final product is used.	The requirements for a textile used for a snowmobile are very different compared to a car seating. As a result, the provider is enabled to conclude several requirements upfront.
F2: Narrowing down customers' requirements	This function demands rough requirements from the customer, which allows the provider for better preparing the co-creation process.	If customers wish an embossing, this allows the provider to conclude that it is a visible textile, as embossing only makes sense when it is visible and not between other layers.
F3: Eliminating unfeasible combinations of properties	This function eliminates combinations of properties that are technically not feasible. This avoids costly, incorrect specifications in an early phase.	Several properties are technically not feasible, e. g., the combination of fire and water resistance. As a result, it is helpful that the artefact does not permit that combination in an early stage.
F4: Anticipating purchase intention	This function allows the provider to anticipate the purchase intention, including asking price, quantity, and timeline.	A co-created product still needs to be sold. This is why the provider benefits from better understanding the willingness to order, and other factors such as the quantity etc.

As shown in *Table 14,* certain functions are linked to each other. For instance, F1 can have a major influence on F3. This also makes the chronological order of the functions important. All of this is deeper described with data from the focus groups in the following *sections.*

4.1 F1: Specifying the final use of the product

The first function refers to the final use of the product. This specification provides information on a variety of factors and determines a series of requirements in the early stage. It was repeatedly pointed out during the focus groups, as this information allows for better preparing the co-creation:

> *Kerstin, Technical Director (provider):*
> *"The first step is always to look at the application purpose. Upholstery for outdoor use is different from car for example. So that's really the first issue the toolkit has to come up with."*

> *Benjamin, Procurement Manager (customer):*
>
> *"The first question I get when we first meet is 'what do you use it for?'. After answering it, the manufacturer suggests solutions along the specific use of the textile, which works out kind of well from my view. [...] Usually, I know the final use for the textile; it's rare that I don't know it myself."*

Another interviewee became clearer when he elaborated on the information needed in the early stage:

> *Janko, Sales Manager (provider):*
>
> *"Only when the customer tells us clearly where the product will be used can we start the co-creation. This information is necessary because it gives us the possibility to see what solutions may work for that customer."*

Knowing the final use not only limits possible solutions, but also allows drawing conclusions on specific requirements that are linked with application purposes. The environment which a product will operate in determines which parameters must be elicited later. For instance, there is a significant difference between different areas that was stressed throughout the focus groups, which can have an impact:

> *Kerstin, Technical Director (provider):*
>
> *"But sometimes the area influences so many things that it is of enormous importance to know the context where the textile should operate in. Textiles used outdoor on cruise ships or indoor in an airplane... I need certain specific requirements here."*

Summing it up, the focus group participants state that specifying the product's final use at an early stage is highly relevant, because it affects numerous factors. Further, the customers inquired find that this is also possible from their perspective. Hence, it is clearly a task that customers are capable to articulate. With regard to its pivotal role, it should be captured at the very beginning, as it has influence on F2 and F3 as shown in *Figure 20*, explained in the following.

4.2 F2: Narrowing down customers' requirements

The second function relates to capturing additional information from the customer, although roughly, which allows the provider to narrow down possible solutions in the early stage. It refers to demands by the customer that are on lower levels of stickiness. In the given context, this could relate to visible properties such as the surface of the textile, e. g. synthetic leather with embossing. Such information is considered helpful for better preparing the co-creation process, which reduces information costs on both sides:

> *Janko, Sales Manager (provider):*
> *"The idea is that we [the salesperson] has a summary on rough customer demands. That would be a great help and lead to a smooth preparation that we usually don't have."*

Also the customer side elaborates on the task what kind of information is articulable:

> *Patrick, Procurement Manager (customer):*
> *"When you are not an expert, you can only assess the 'visible' qualities. So yes, I could select some basic design how the textile 'should look like' in a toolkit, if this is relevant to that textile."*

However, which specifications the customer may provide here depends on the context in which the product would finally operate. For instance, several textiles are non-visible in their context, e. g. when built between textile layers. For them, it does not make sense to specify aesthetics. As a result, in some cases, F2 builds upon the final product use of F1, as indicated by the arrow in *Figure 20.*

Another point that the focus group participants mentioned concerns a free text form. There, customers can freely enter additional information. This is regarded useful because providers receive more information on peculiarities from the customer:

> *Bert, CEO (provider):*
>
> *"It is great to get any useful hint from the customer on the design, the precise final use, colors or just anything. Sometimes one word is enough. My favorite example is 'snowmobile seat'. Just that single information allows us to grasp dozens of specific requirements, without any direct interaction with the customer."*

4.3 F3: Eliminating unfeasible combinations of properties

A lot of specifications are only relevant in certain applications. In addition, certain property combinations are technically not feasible. As a result, it makes sense to eliminate irrelevant and unfeasible ones when selecting the final use.

> *Kerstin, Technical Director (provider):*
>
> *"Many areas place very different demands on the textile. The one, for example, in the normal area needs to be hard-wearing [car seating], but must not be UV-resistant or cold-resistant. Boat imitation leather on the other hand must be UV-resistant, must not get moldy, but doesn't need to be cold-resistant."*

Similar to narrowing down customers' requirements, the elimination of unfeasible or irrelevant properties can also be based on the final product application (see arrow from F1 to F3 in *Figure 20*). Taking this one step further, the selection of properties not only suggests appropriate specifications, but also allows the provider to eliminate inappropriate ones. This is why only the provider is linked to F3, shown in *Figure 20.* The same principle applies to combining certain properties that are either unfeasible or pointless, such as the combination of, e. g., two conflicting requirements 'flame resistance' and 'water resistance'. Focus group participants see a great benefit to eliminate several properties according to the final use or other selected features in an early phase. This function serves to avoid technically unfeasible customer demands that are automatically prevented.

> *Benno, Sales Manager (provider):*
> *"For us, it is decisive that unfeasible combinations don't get into the process. We must eliminate them as early as possible. [...] Ideally, the customer doesn't even have the opportunity to select unfeasible combinations."*

This approach is to some extent also implemented in other systems used by some of the researched companies:

> *Anja, Head of Sales (provider):*
> *"We use like a drop-down list that shows what properties are available for one option. But this is not for the customer. We should use something like that also for our customers."*

It is expected that the elimination of unfeasible property combinations facilitates the whole specification procedure. At the same time, incorrect specifications are prevented from the start, which can increase efficiency and entail cost savings for both provider and customer.

4.4 F4: Anticipating purchase intention

Another interesting function was encountered in the data that refers to customers' eventual willingness to order the co-created product. Besides the specification of the final use and properties, all concerning the high-tech product itself, the providers stress the need for further information to grasp whether the customer would buy the co-created product in the end. Allowing providers to perform a rough organizational calculation upfront is vital to assess whether the final product is sellable. This is particularly relevant for high-tech products because personal co-creation sessions are time-consuming and require high interaction costs (Madhavaram & Appan, 2010). Moreover, such co-creation projects can span over a couple of years. Before starting the co-creation, it must be appraised beforehand if there is a basis for efficient and successful solution development. Conversely, providers seem to be regularly confronted with discovering that a product is not producible for the asking price provided by the customer – in later stages. As a result, it is of relevance to ensure that the customer provides his purchase intention that allows a rough organizational calculation upfront:

> *Hans, Senior Development Manager (provider):*
> *"We must get an idea about the expected financial expectations overall. Let's say business case expectations from the customer [...]. We must understand how many meters the customer will probably buy, and what the asking price is."*

Throughout the focus groups, practitioners expressed a necessity to anticipate the purchase intention from the customer at an early stage, which ideally includes approximated quantity and the asking price. This need is useful for an initial appraisal of financial capabilities and scale.

> *Benno, Sales Manager (provider):*
> *"You try to get some information about financial capability, and whether they are planning to buy in the end. And if the asking price is very low, we can directly say 'no'."*

As a result, it makes sense to collect such information to identify market opportunities right from the start. Both provider and customer are expected to profit from this function, because it is also in the interest of customers that their expectations are accurately assessed by the provider. As such additional information is only assessable in connection with the rough product specification, this information is requested at last.

5 Demonstrating the toolkit

After some iteration, the final version of the artefact with its four described functions was translated into a toolkit. While it addresses the four functions of the artefact, it seeks to minimize the effort for the customer with a clear structure. The toolkit is demonstrated for one of the participating companies by using their decision tree and product portfolio data. This allows the evaluation part to present a toolkit fed with real-life data, and to gather valuable data from the interviewees as they are presented a non-abstract toolkit with their known company data.

The provider where the toolkit was demonstrated co-creates high-tech fabrics with specific functions. For instance, the textiles are tear-proof, heat-resistant, and cold-resistant, and have customized embossments. One example for their use is upholstery for mobility. On the one hand, they are installed as interior upholstery in airplanes and cars. On the other hand, they are used outdoor for motorcycle or snowmobile seats. All of them pose very different requirements, for instance regarding their resistance to heat or cold.

The architecture of the toolkit follows a modular approach that demands the required information from F1 – F4 step by step with the abovementioned artefact functions, presented in the use case diagram in *Figure 20.* The artefact-based toolkit is demonstrated in *Figure 21.* Afterwards it is elaborated on its design.

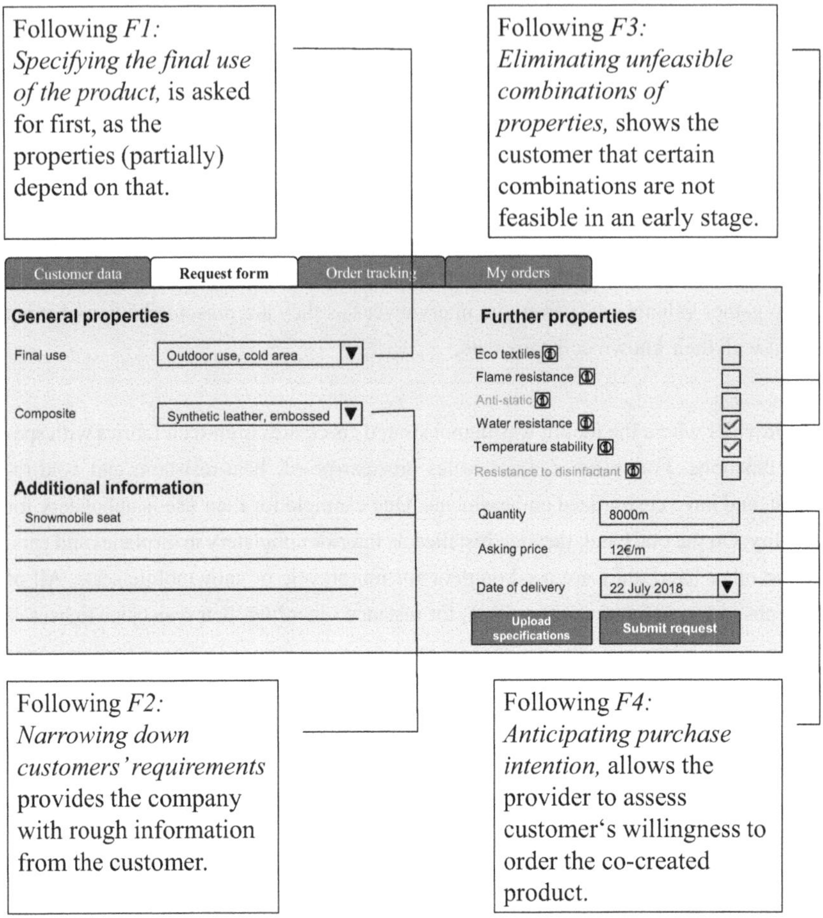

Figure 21: Presentation of the artefact-based toolkit for the focal company[33]

[33] Due to confidentiality reasons, drop-down lists and further information cannot be shown as this would disclose sensitive company data such as the firm-specific decision tree.

F1: Specifying the final use of the product. The first information to collect is the final use of the product, see 'final use' in *Figure 21*. A drop-down list retrieves the final use from the customer. Simple terminology enables the customer to easily select the option of choice. In the given context, the customer opts for 'outdoor use, cold area'. Based on that, the toolkit adjusts the available options in the drop-down list of 'composite' (also linked to F2). Furthermore, it directly eliminates certain options (also linked to F3) on the right hand site, below 'further properties'. The given example eliminates two properties, shown by the grey font in *Figure 21*. As a result, unfeasible combinations are avoided in this early stage.

F2: Narrowing down customers' requirements. In order to capture additional information, F2 aims at collecting rough information by the customer. In the given example, for 'composite', the customer selected 'synthetic leather, embossed'. This allows the provider to conclude several properties upfront, for instance the provider can anticipate that the customer wishes a visible textile, as embossing only makes sense when textiles are visible. Further, in the free text, the customer entered 'snowmobile seat', which would enable the provider to further narrow down customers' requirements and to better prepare the subsequent face-to-face interaction.

F3: Eliminating unfeasible combinations of properties. The toolkit shows that the selection of some parameters automatically eliminates others (e. g. choosing 'water resistance' as a requirement automatically eliminates the option 'resistance to disinfectant'). Likewise, as the demonstration of F1 and F2 have already shown, unfeasible properties are also eliminated on the basis of the specified final use of the product (see F1), or based on customers' rough requirements (see F2). That information enables the provider to derive technical specifications such as required technologies or the equipment of the textile.

F4: Anticipating purchase intention. As the toolkit shows, three dates are retrieved that allow the provider to better understand customers' willingness to order: desired quantity, asking price and date of delivery.

6 Evaluating the artefact

In general, the toolkit was considered useful by the practitioners to reduce the information costs. A closer look at the four functions of the artefact, however, allows a more differentiated assessment of how the toolkit can lower information costs in their daily work in co-creating with customers. The evaluation reports on seven in-depth interviews conducted in the focal company. It gathered insights from both the provider and customer perspective.

6.1 F1: Specifying the final use of the product

F1 was regarded an essential feature especially by the interviewees from the provider's side in the evaluation. Consistently, it was stressed that it makes sense that the toolkit retrieves information on the final use at first. Like in the design and artefact development phase, the interviewees stressed that this is a key information that determines various factors, such as quality requirements or stakeholders to involve in the subsequent face-to-face interaction. In line with the suggested order of the functions, it was stated:

> *Anja, Head of Sales (provider):*
> *"It is ideal to put the final use first. The best solution is that the customer only has one choice to make at the beginning, and nothing else: the final use. Then, the toolkit adapts all the other options according to that."*

Another interviewee stated with his management perspective on the topic:

> *Bert, CEO (provider):*
> *"I can also determine the required expert from my team that is responsible for that co-creation, when I know where the product will be used finally. [...] It facilitates the whole process to know that before we meet up first."*

Furthermore, as the quotes indicate, the final use allows the provider to narrow down customers' requirements based on the final use (see F2) and to eliminate unfeasible combinations (see F3). As a result, retrieving the final use first is very useful from the provider's view. When looking at the customer perspective, it is more relevant whether the customers are capable of articulating the required information. Also, it needs to be asked whether they are willing to reveal it. For both, data do not show problems with that:

> *Benjamin, Procurement Manager (customer):*
> *"I like the different choices here. Because I can easily understand what they want here, and I'm not asked too difficult issues. I think I can answer that in any case."*

Some other interviews exhibit reasons why customers are sometimes unwilling to unveil several requirements in the early phase, for instance because this would allow the provider to anticipate the customer's customer:

> *Petra, Strategic Purchaser (customer):*
> *"Sometimes I don't want that the manufacturer knows exactly where the product is used. For instance, I don't want to say that it will be an airplane seating, especially not in this early phase when I'm not familiar with the manufacturer yet. But the way it is presented here [in the toolkit], I don't see any problem to specify it."*

6.2 F2: Narrowing down customers' requirements

Apart from the factors linked to the final use, various additional factors can be roughly decided upon with the help of the toolkit. As the example in the toolkit shows, one choice made by the customer relates to aesthetics. With that information, providers state that they are enabled to conclude that it is a visible textile which narrows down several customer requirements. Based on that, both the provider and the customer save costs as they invest less time later on:

Hans, Senior Development Manager (provider):

"I don't want to exaggerate; but it's a dream to start in a joint development project with that much information. I would say we could skip two initial meetings. Yes, indeed, that information you show here in the toolkit would be typically captured during two meetings with the customer. And just that word 'snowmobile' helps us so much, it would be terrific to always have such information."

Data also show that it is useful to better prepare the face-to-face interaction by involving appropriate experts from the providing company:

Bert, CEO (provider):

"And then we can work with that [information gathered by the toolkit] and then there isn't this back and forth changing all the time. For example, I know for the very first meeting what stakeholders I must bring together."

As a result, F2 is also linked to F3, eliminating certain options for the textile properties. This was supported in the data, including both procurement and sales managers. Giving customers only the available options reduces information costs for the overall co-creation process, as it can be better prepared.

However, although the free text has advantages, the evaluation of F2 showed one concern in this regard. Customers may tend to overload the free text with less relevant information. Both customers and providers indicated that threat:

Hanno, Procurement Manger (customer):

"Sure, when I'm uncertain what's relevant, I just upload everything that I have. That could be the problem when I don't know exactly what information is relevant for the manufacturer."

This is also clearly stated by several providers. Putting it clearly, data exhibit doubts whether this form is capable of preventing an information overload by the customer. While structuring most of the required information, the toolkit still offers room for the unassisted upload of free text. Apparently, customers frequently communicate irrelevant details as a strategy to avoid a lack of relevant information. This seems to be the case especially for less experienced customers:

> *Horst, Technical Director (provider):*
> *"I would fear that inexperienced customers would just feed that platform with everything that they have even though it's not relevant. And the result would be that we end up viewing tons of information, and then we don't save time in the end."*

This problem indicates a trade-off between flexibility and structure. Although allowing customers to upload additional pieces of information themselves can be beneficial by drastically reducing information costs, it also holds the danger of losing its advantages. The problem illustrates the necessity of combining structure with flexibility when co-creating high-tech products. Besides, structuring the specifications that are required can encourage the customer to take necessary decisions instead of postponing them.

6.3 F3: Eliminating unfeasible combinations of properties

The toolkit not only allows making first choices, but also aims to eliminate unfeasible combinations in an early phase. The evaluation of F1 and F2 already showed certain advantages of F3. The following paragraphs focus on the evaluation of F3 that is not related to F1 and F2.

When showing the toolkit to the providers, they stressed that F3 reduces the threat that customers come up with unfeasible combinations of properties. As expressed in the interviews, the involved stakeholders often face a gap between customer wishes and provider's capabilities.

> *Anja, Head of Sales (provider):*
>
> *"Or if the customer... what often is the case, the customer wants something that is not possible from our side. With that system [the toolkit] we would avoid most of these requests early."*

Another interviewee from the providing side clearly emphasizes the provider's responsibility to take care of the overall process in light of F3:

> *Janko, Sales Manager (provider):*
>
> *"This function is great to avoid that unfeasible combinations get into the actual co-creation process. This is costly and also very frustrating for everyone involved. Imagine you travel far, meet up and find out that it was all a waste of time. [...] I also see it as our [provider's] task to check very early whether it makes sense to meet up, because I also need to take care of my customer relationship."*

The evaluation of F3 shows that the difference between what the customer expects and what the provider is actually capable to deliver used to be a problem that was encountered in the face-to-face interaction. With the toolkit, this is solved earlier. This saves costs and avoids frustration on both sites.

6.4 F4: Anticipating purchase intention

F4 was set up to better assess whether the customer will eventually buy the co-created product. Primarily, providers emphasized its usefulness when they were shown the toolkit. For instance, they stated that this function allows them to directly reject some customer requests when customers' demands are not realizable:

Kerstin, Technical Director (provider):

"Especially customer's asking price astonishes us sometimes. It makes a lot of sense that the toolkit asks for a rough number. Just to get an idea what the customer has in mind. Sometimes it is so low that we can reject it right away, so it would save us a lot of time."

Further, the customers also stated that they are open to reveal such information, although it is not a mandatory field in the toolkit:

Patrick, Procurement Manager (customer):

"I can understand why the manufacturer wants to know that. I would provide that information, why not? It doesn't hurt me and helps the provider. [...] Also, if my [asking] price is totally off, it's ok that we don't follow up on a joint project, so it's also good for me."

Besides these advantages, the providers found that it is useful to get such customer information in a written form, as this is regarded to foster commitment. Hence, the written form was clearly preferred over information on the phone or in person:

Hans, Sales Manager (provider):

"The toolkit has the advantage that the information is always in written form. This is something that we can later use as a discussion basis that the customer already agreed on. It is also nice that the customer must think of such issues in an early stage."

For concluding this *section*, the four functions of the toolkit proved useful for capturing information on lower levels of stickiness in high-tech product co-creation. In essence, the toolkit performs the task of conciliating expectations and requirements from both customer's and provider's side, while at the same time eliminating cases in which they cannot be brought together. In total, it is argued for the usefulness of the artefact as it reduces information costs on both sides customer and provider in an early stage.

7 Conclusions

This study in *Part IV* reported on designing an artefact that allows better preparing the face-to-face co-creation of high-tech products in the German textile industry. This is useful to reduce information costs for customer and provider. Drawing upon five focus groups, an artefact with four functions was set up. The artefact aims to capture information on lower levels of stickiness in high-tech product co-creation. Following DSR, the artefact was translated into a toolkit and demonstrated. It was set up along the specific product portfolio of one company. Seven interviews served to evaluate the artefact, involving both the customer and provider view on the artefact. The findings suggest that the artefact-based toolkit is useful for lowering information costs by a better preparation of the subsequent face-to-face interaction.

This study exhibits an individual contribution to research, managerial implications as well as limitations presented in the following *sections*. An overarching discussion of the empirical studies is then provided in *Part V*.

7.1 Contribution to research

The study's theoretical contribution is two-fold. First, it adds valuable insights to the field of B2B co-creation (Anderson & Wynstra, 2010; La Rocca et al., 2016). In particular, the findings relate to the highly complex ETO context, in which the solution space is not defined upfront, which widely disqualifies present configurator approaches (Gilmore & Pine, 1997). Despite some studies stating that toolkit usage is quite limited in the high-tech domain (Fauska et al., 2014; Laage-Hellman et al., 2014), an innovative B2B toolkit is demonstrated that is based on an artefact developed using DSR (Peffers & Tuunanen, 2007). Relating to calls for further research on tools which support effective co-creation (Barczak, 2012; Frow et al., 2015), its design provides fruitful insights into mastering product complexity with toolkits. Second, the study contributes to the elicitation of sticky information on lower levels (Ogawa, 1998; von Hippel, 1990b). This is considered fundamental for being able to start off the co-creation of rather complex offerings (Aarikka-Stenroos & Jaakkola, 2012). The study thereby answers the question as to which specifications are both on lower level stickiness and still useful for the provider in the co-creation of high-tech products.

7.2 Managerial implications

Informed by focus groups and interviews with practitioners, a toolkit was built with a strong application orientation. For managers, this expands the understanding on how co-creation processes can be better designed as these findings help companies to support the face-to-face interaction by allowing for a better preparation upfront for both customer and provider.

According to the data, toolkits with the identified functions provide a structure that helps focus the face-to-face interaction by interlinking the involved stakeholders and their expectations more closely with each other. For instance, toolkit approaches as proposed serve to filter out unfeasible requests in the early stages. This research demonstrates that a toolkit with the identified functions is capable of meeting the challenge of bridging the gap between the customer's expectations and the provider's capabilities, which is often a problem. It is argued that the suggested benefit of a pre-specification of requirements is likely to hold true also for other tasks touching upon high product complexity.

7.3 Limitations & further research

Following a design-oriented approach that is to some extent tailored to the specific conditions in the examined industry, the findings of this study are subject to a threefold limitation. First, this research is focused on the German high-tech industry, in which haptic features are of particular importance. Consequently, the results are rather applicable to industries that also require face-to-face interaction throughout the co-creation process. Further research is needed to examine which of the described functions and benefits of the toolkit can be transferred to other B2B contexts that dispense with face-to-face co-creation. Second, although the interviewed procurement managers were well-placed to take the customer's perspective, it might in addition be fruitful to enrich the information base with richer customer insight. Finally, the implementation remained limited to a visual representation without technical realization in the company's existing information technology landscape. As a consequence, further research and testing should involve the technical implementation of the toolkit in order to complement this study's findings with insights into its operational handling within productive environments.

Part V – Summary and implications

L. K. Grafmüller, *Co-Creation of High-Tech Products in the B2B Domain*,
Markt- und Unternehmensentwicklung Markets and Organisations,
https://doi.org/10.1007/978-3-658-28412-1_5

1 Summary of studies

This dissertation examines the co-creation of high-tech products in the B2B domain. In the era of open innovation, this research targets a topic of both practical and academic relevance. The overall objective of this dissertation is a better understanding of the phenomenon which appears reasonable as extant literature on the topic is rather scarce. Following a series of calls for more empirical work, three studies are undertaken to approach the topic from different angles, involving co-creating customers and providers of the high-tech B2B domain. Eventually, *Part V* summarizes and discusses the findings of the empirical studies, as the embedding shows in *Figure 22*.

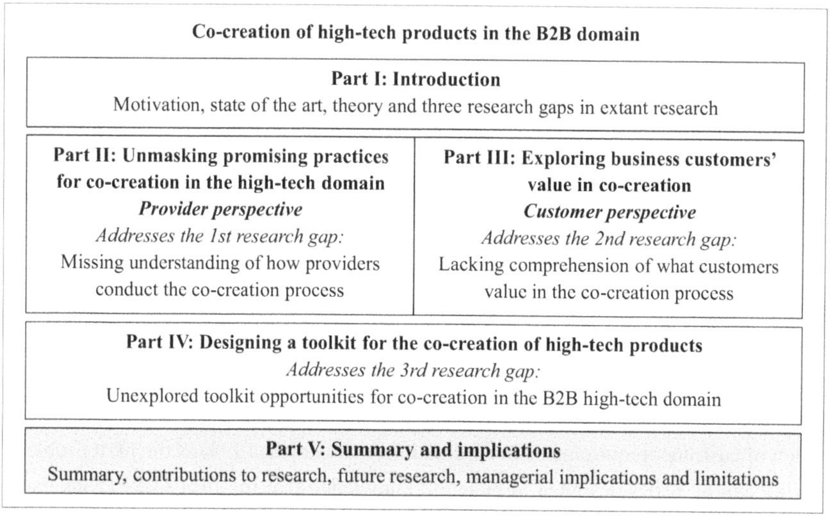

Figure 22: Embedding of *Part V* in the dissertation

This *part* commences with an overall summary and discussions of the empirical work, followed by brief individual summaries of each study. Then, the contribution to research of this dissertation is presented. This is complemented by two avenues for further research. An overview of managerial implications follows. Eventually, the conclusion includes the limitations as well as the final notes.

Since the research gaps are tackled by three empirical studies in an independent way, it makes sense to elaborate on them in a joint summary. To start off, *Part II* explores how providers conduct the co-creation process with their customers. It is detailed how customers are managed and involved in co-creating high-tech products. The results of *Part II* are four promising practices that providers have gradually evolved to successfully conduct co-creation processes with business customers. Now focusing on the other side in co-creation, *Part III* analyzes what business customers value in the co-creation process, which is decisive for proper customer engagement. Besides the acknowledged functional value in extant research (e. g. Eggert & Ulaga, 2002), the empirical study sheds light on the neglected areas of emotional and social value. This delivers profound insight in customer's motivation and process drivers to engage in co-creation. With these two empirical studies, both parties involved in the joint development process were examined. This allows for mutually mirroring the validity of the findings as both co-creation camps express similar topics.

Integrating *Part IV,* this design-oriented study aims to point out opportunities for the usage of toolkits to enhance the efficiency and efficacy of co-creating high-tech products. While extant research advises to use only rich media such as face-to-face when products are rather complex (Fauska et al., 2014; Laage-Hellman et al., 2014), an attempt is undertaken to build a novel toolkit approach. While *Part II* and *Part III* focus on the process to face high levels of sticky information (von Hippel, 1994), *Part IV* raises the question how lower levels of sticky information can be captured with a toolkit. Summing it up, from a problem-solving perspective, the three studies enhance the elicitation of customer requirements in co-creation (von Hippel, 1994) as the joint problem solving can be better designed to generate knowledge that the firm seeks (Nickerson & Zenger, 2004).

After interweaving the three studies, the overall value of this research is assessed below. To do this, the structure follows the four dimensions by Lincoln and Guba (1985) in order to establish trustworthiness. For qualitative research, Huff (2009, p. 32) describes these four dimensions as follows:

(1) *Credibility* denotes the degree to which data reflect the results.

(2) *Transferability* relates to the appropriateness of the findings for other contexts.

(3) *Dependability* describes the degree to which data remain consistent with regard to time, place, and situation.

(4) *Confirmability* assesses the degree to which results can be traced back to data, showing no investigator bias.

Table 15 provides an overview along these four dimensions. All empirical studies are taken into consideration for an overarching assessment of the value of the research:

Table 15: Overview of qualitative research assessment based on Huff (2009, p. 32)

Quality criterion	In this research
Credibility	- The author of this dissertation has been collaborating more than three years with the German textile industry, which has been his core task in a research project over the last years[34]. - Data collection and analysis was done by the author. - Preliminary results were mirrored with managers involved in co-creation at mid-term in a 90 minute workshop that included more than 30 company representatives of the German textile industry. - Final results were discussed and evaluated at a one-day workshop with participating interviewees. - Different data sources were used (e. g. field notes, workshops for result mirroring, follow-up interviews, and internal firm documents).
Transferability	- In total, 68 companies were visited and interviewed that face high complexity in co-creation processes.
Dependability	- Data were collected in 68 different, independent textile companies. - Findings show similar challenges that the companies face regarding complex offerings. - Limitations exist regarding the qualitative research design, because interviews may represent an extract of current challenges.
Confirmability	- Results were mirrored with both informants and surveyed co-creators in several workshops.

[34] The author of this dissertation started the company collaboration in the German textile industry in May 2015 within the scope of the research project *futureTEX*, funded by the BMBF (FKZ: 03ZZ0604A; 03ZZ0618B).

1.1 Summary of Part II: Promising practices

Part II unmasks promising practices that show how providers conduct the co-creation process of high-tech products. With the ever-greater product complexity, this understanding is considered crucial. Taking a problem-solving perspective, three co-creation challenges in the high-tech domain were depicted from extant literature: *time intensity, requirement capturing* and *customer engagement*. An explorative approach within the German textile industry was undertaken to identify promising practices that providers use to tackle these challenges. 29 interviews with managers involved in co-creating high-tech products were analyzed. Four promising practices were unmasked: (1) *Building an open and trustful relationship* includes demonstrations of the importance of customer's knowledge, the emphasis of a joint learning process and the disclosure of product data to build trust; (2) *avoiding incorrect specification* encompasses, inter alia, deep explaining and the invitation of customer's customers. (3) *Adapting to different customer types* refers to the bipolarity of design-oriented and efficiency-driven customers, which need to be integrated fundamentally different; (4) *creating physical spaces* comprises the organization of an 'Innovation Day' and using boundary objects. The study is concluded by an individual contribution to research, managerial implications and limitations. *Table 16* provides an overview of *Part II*.

Table 16: Summary of Part II

Study	**Part II – Unmasking promising practices for co-creation in the high-tech domain**
Need	More and more B2B companies involve customers in the co-creation of high-tech products. Especially the correct elicitation of customer requirements, including sticky information, is promising. However, literature is scarce on current practices of the co-creation of high-tech products.
Research question	What practices enable firms to successfully manage and involve customers in the co-creation of high-tech products?
Method used	Exploratory qualitative interview study, analyzed using 1st order concepts and 2nd order themes to unmask also process details
Sample	29 semi-structured interviews with actors mainly involved in co-creating high-tech products from the provider side
Findings	Four promising practices are unmasked: - Building an open and trustful relationship - Avoiding incorrect specification - Adapting to different customer types - Creating physical spaces The promising practices are detailed in-depth and brought into context of co-creating high-tech products.
Contribution	Following several calls for further research, this study answers a series of questions in the field of co-creation research. It helps translate current theoretical insights into actionable knowledge by identifying four promising practices that have gradually evolved by high-tech providers.
Implications	The study delivers useful advice how to design co-creation activities that target high-tech product development.
Future research	Findings suggest adapting to different customer types: strikingly, one type values emotional and social value within the co-creation process. This is novel to B2B research. As this study targets the provider side only, another study should focus on inquiring the customer to gather unfiltered information.

1.2 Summary of Part III: Customers' value

Focusing on the second research gap, *Part III* explores business customers' value in co-creation. Understanding the customer value is crucial to properly engage the customer along his preferences. The proper engagement decides whether customers are motivated and willing to participate in problem-solving activities. Based on reviewing related literature, it is argued that only few studies focus on what business customers actually value in co-creation processes. While research heavily stresses the importance of functional value, more recent studies indicate the importance of emotional and social value. To deeper explain emotional and social value, *Part II* examines such value components in co-creation processes in B2B. 42 business customers of high-tech products in the high-tech textile industry in Germany were inquired. Co-creating high-tech products often involves actors with an engineering background as a high degree of technical expertise is required, which is why the focus is on this domain. The results emphasize the importance of social and emotional value: for instance, the value *openness* is prerequisite for co-creating high-tech products with business customers. Moreover, data reveals the decisive role of emotional value components *playfulness* and *self-fulfillment*. Such value components are novel to B2B research, which yields major consequences for co-creating with business customers. It is argued for major consequences in several regards and the contribution to research, managerial implications and future research are formulated. *Part III* is summarized in *Table 17*.

Table 17: Summary of Part III

Study	Part III – Exploring business customers' value in co-creation
Need	In order to have motivated customers in co-creation activities, the customer value of the co-creation process must be understood. The majority of the studies stresses the importance of functional value. However, recent studies indicate that emotional and social value is important for business customers, too. For providers, it is requisite to understand also these values to properly engage customers in joint problem solving.
Research question	What emotional & social value components play a role in B2B co-creation with high product complexity?
Method used	Exploratory qualitative interview study, analyzed using a thematic content analysis to explain motives and underlying concepts in-depth
Sample	42 customers of high-tech products, often engaged and experienced in co-creation
Findings	Three value components in the area of social and emotional value are identified and described. - *Openness* describes the customers' demand of the provider to be open. - *Playfulness* relates to customers' desire to play with different technologies, which does not necessarily correspond with the actual goal. - *Self-fulfillment* describes customers' emotional satisfaction and pride in contributing to the development of a novel, high-tech product.
Contribution	This study delivers empirical evidence that business customers do not only value functional value, but also social and emotional value. This is striking as business customers are acknowledged to act, most notably, rationally.
Implications	An urgent implication stems of the existence of playfulness and self-fulfillment in B2B co-creation, because the co-creation processes need to be designed accordingly to benefit from motivated customers.
Future research	Adding significant insights to this field, it seems promising to integrate the findings in established product development processes.

1.3 Summary of Part IV: Opportunities for toolkits

Part IV points out opportunities for the usage of toolkits to enhance the efficiency of the co-creation of high-tech products. Tackling the third research gap, it aims at building an artefact that is tested and evaluated in a real-life setting. The need emerges from the acknowledgement that high-tech products need to be co-created in personal and time-consuming interactions to capture the high levels of sticky information. Although being very costly, research suggests a consensus that such offerings are co-created most smoothly in face-to-face settings. However, opportunities to capture lower levels of sticky information have not been explored in the context of high-tech product co-creation – and this information is typically also part of the required information. Also rising the question what information on lower level stickiness is helpful for the provider, a toolkit is set up in cooperation with B2B companies of the German high-tech textile industry. Using DSR, an artefact is built informed by five focus groups with 20 participants in total. The artefact is a use case diagram that exhibits four functions. For instance, the function *specifying the final use of the product* is first, as it comes with implications for the overall process. Then, for one of the companies, an artefact-based toolkit is demonstrated along the company's specific product portfolio specifications and its decision tree. The iterative evaluation process is informed by seven in-depth interviews to help describe how the toolkit captures lower levels of sticky information in the co-creation of high-tech products. Suchlike toolkit approaches are novel as they deal with undefined solution spaces, for which the contribution and managerial implications are presented. The limitations and avenues for future research are delineated to conclude the study. *Table 18* summarizes *Part IV*.

Table 18: Overview of Part IV

Study	Part IV – Designing a toolkit for the co-creation of high-tech products
Need	Often, the information costs are very high in the co-creation of high-tech products. Acknowledging that high levels of sticky information must be elicited in face-to-face settings, it appears fruitful to examine lower levels of sticky information that are ascertainable with a toolkit. In research, such approaches have not been analyzed in the context of high product complexity. In this regard, it must be understood what specifications are both articulable by the customer by using a toolkit and helpful for the provider.
Research question	What sticky information on lower levels is helpful for the provider and how can it be captured with a toolkit?
Method used	With a design-oriented method, an artefact is built and evaluated. Its collaborative and iterative development is informed by focus groups and interviews.
Sample	Five focus groups; seven interviews with both customer and provider perspective within one company
Findings	For the use case diagram, four functions were identified that foster the efficiency of the co-creation process: - F1: Specifying the final use of the product - F2: Pre-specifying the required information - F3: Eliminating unfeasible combinations of properties - F4: Anticipating purchase intention These functions are translated into a toolkit evaluated in a real-life context. It is explained how the face-to-face interaction can be better prepared with the information gathered by the toolkit.
Contribution	The findings underpin how information costs can be lowered with the usage of a toolkit, as the face-to-face interaction can be better prepared.
Implications	The study suggests for practitioners that toolkits with the identified functions help focus the subsequent face-to-face interaction by interlinking the involved stakeholders and their expectations more closely with each other.
Future research	This study is based on a rather small sample of only seven interviews, however covering all stakeholders in touch with co-creation in the focal company. Future research should address the topic on a larger scale.

2 Contribution to research

This *chapter* presents the contributions derived from the three empirical studies. The first *section* presents the contributions to co-creation research with special emphasis on the B2B high-tech domain, then, the second *section* focuses on contributions to the problem-solving literature with a focus on sticky information.

2.1 Contribution to co-creation in the B2B high-tech domain

As the development of new products and services is vital to a company's competitiveness, this research contributes to an ongoing debate in innovation research (Achilladelis et al., 1971; Cui & Wu, 2017). The overall contribution to co-creation research concerns the conduct of the face-to-face interaction between the customer and provider for joint product development (Geyer et al., 2018). Such processes are described in a detailed way to provide valuable insights. The focus on the face-to-face interaction is particularly insightful, as recent research rather puts emphasis on web-enabled co-creation (Möslein, 2013; Nambisan et al., 2017; Piller et al., 2017), for instance in innovation contests (see e. g. Haller et al., 2011). Therefore, the findings of this dissertation help understand how sticky information is better elicited in the face-to-face process (von Hippel, 1994).

Moving to the contributions specific to the B2B high-tech domain, this dissertation follows numerous calls for further research in the B2B domain on co-creation, for instance on co-creation practices (Frow et al., 2015; Perks et al., 2012; Tidd & Bessant, 2018), on studies that focus on the joint development process (Kohtamäki & Rajala, 2016; La Rocca et al., 2016; Salomonson et al., 2012), rather complex offerings (La Rocca et al., 2016; Madhavaram & Appan, 2010; Olausson & Berggren, 2012; Suh, 2005), the neglected customer perspective in co-creation (Mustak et al., 2013; Petri & Jacob, 2016; Randhawa et al., 2016; Roberts et al., 2014), and on actionable knowledge in co-creation research (Baumann & Le Meunier-FitzHugh, 2014; Grönroos & Ravald, 2011).

The contributions to research relate to three points of interest[35], showcased in *Figure 23*. These points are deeper depicted in the following.

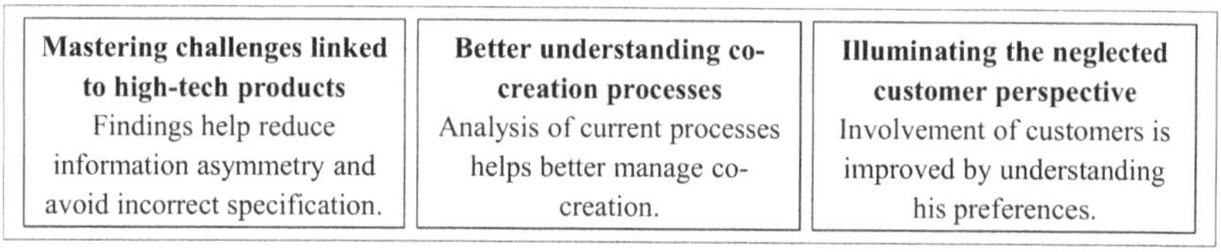

Figure 23: Three main contributions to co-creation in the high-tech B2B domain

The first contribution refers to *mastering challenges linked to high-tech products.* Such high-tech products are high cost and often customized components, whose development frequently results in cost overruns, time delays and eventually stakeholder dissatisfaction (Hobday & Rush, 1999; Nightingale, 2000; Olausson & Berggren, 2010). This dissertation contributes to this challenge in three major regards. First, co-creating high-tech products requires *"controlled flexibility"* (Olausson & Berggren, 2010, p. 383), which means that development processes need to be *"quasi-formalized"* (ibid., p. 395). This dissertation builds on the works by these authors as it adds insight on how this quasi-formalization is achieved, e. g., by organizing a hackathon for jointly developing high-tech products. Second, high-tech product development is often linked to a high degree of uncertainty perceived by the customer and to a significant information asymmetry (Aarikka-Stenroos & Jaakkola, 2012; Alejandro et al., 2011; La Rocca et al., 2016). This research offers manifold answers on the question how information asymmetries are bridged. Overall, it is showcased how high product complexity is faced in co-creation. It is argued that this contribution is gaining more and more importance because technological complexity is constantly rising in numerous industries (Graevenitz et al., 2011; Jacob & Ulaga, 2008; La Rocca et al., 2016; Möller, 2006). Third, a contribution is made to avoid incorrect specification by suggesting both concrete practices and an artefact-based toolkit. This follows the works by Hobday (1998), Nightingale (2000), Olausson and Berggren (2010) and La Rocca et al. (2016). With the findings provided in this dissertation, high-tech product development processes with their

[35] For a detailed overview of the literature, see *Part I, Chapter 2* referring to the state of the art in current research and the detection of the three research gaps in extant literature. This chapter also deduces the relevance and urgency of the research at hand.

current challenges are better understood. Several approaches to tackle them are delivered, as well as concrete activities to avoid incorrect specification.

The second contribution is about *better understanding co-creation processes.* It is argued that the three empirical studies significantly expand the understanding *how* the co-creation of high-tech products with business customers is managed, structured and organized. This contributes to the innovation research priority formulated by Biemans and Langerak (2015), asking how companies manage the involvement of customers in product development. Further, all studies extent the work from La Rocca et al. (2016) as they add deep insight into joint development processes of rather complex products in the B2B domain. Further, it is argued that the findings have led to relevant discoveries (Kohtamäki & Rajala, 2016). Also in this vein, looking at current practices of high-tech product co-creation, this dissertation provides insight into detailed activities, and builds on the work by Trischler et al. (2017), stating that co-creation processes are still a *"black box"* in their recent study (ibid., p. 265). Moreover, the dissertation follows several calls to focus on the joint development process, as this is often neglected in the empirical part despite its importance (La Rocca et al., 2016; Laage-Hellman et al., 2014; Salomonson et al., 2012; Vargo & Lusch, 2008). Further, this research confirms that putting the emphasis on the process is so decisive in co-creation, as the overall success depends on it (Cui & Wu, 2017; Malshe & Friend, 2018; Roberts et al., 2014). Summing it up, the knowledge generated in this dissertation helps improve the customer engagement as well as the design of according co-creation processes. This is in line with a number of recent calls (Barczak, 2012; Frow et al., 2015; La Rocca et al., 2016; Malshe & Friend, 2018; Vaquero Martín et al., 2016).

The third contribution refers to *illuminating the neglected customer perspective.* This contribution follows works demanding a stronger focus on the customer as his needs are at the center in co-creation (Malshe & Friend, 2018; Payne et al., 2008; Petri & Jacob, 2016). With the present research, a contribution is made toward a better understanding of the customer motives to engage him properly. On the one hand, the results add deeper insight to the seminal work of Prior (2013) who stresses the importance of emotional and social value in B2B. This dissertation confirms the importance of these value components. Nonetheless, the existence of social and emotional value has been in contrast to extant B2B research, typically describing business customers as functionally-driven (e. g. Eggert & Ulaga, 2002). As a result, it is argued that the findings of this research extend the work in a field that has been widely neglected in B2B research (Füller et al., 2010; La Rocca et al., 2016; Malshe & Friend, 2018; Mustak et al., 2013). Moreover, the findings contribute to a better conceptualization of value in B2B, which needs to catch up with the advanced B2C context (Arslanagic-Kalajdzic & Zabkar, 2017; Candi & Kahn, 2016; Prior, 2013). On the other hand, the understanding of promising practices as well as the customer value of the co-creation process helps enhance the topic of customer engagement. As extant literature suggests a consensus that the co-creation success fundamentally relies on customer engagement (Hakanen & Jaakkola, 2012; Jaakkola & Alexander, 2014; La Rocca et al., 2016), the findings enhance the understanding and allow for improving the customer engagement in the B2B domain. To conclude, the research at hand demonstrates that the statement *"It's all B2B"* by Vargo and Lusch (2011, p. 181) is much too broad in scope for the context of high-tech product co-creation: business customers need to be involved in very different ways and their motivation to engage deviates.

2.2 Contribution to problem-solving and sticky information

The problem-solving literature often raises the question *"how a manager should organize individuals to generate knowledge that the firm seeks"* (Nickerson & Zenger, 2004, p. 618). This dissertation adds at least three responses to that question in the context of co-creating high-tech products.

First, the co-creation of high-tech products is an ill-structured task, for which Simon (1973) suggests that information seekers develop *"possible programs (strategies)"*[36] to face the complexity involved (Simon, 1978, p. 273). These *"possible programs"* are identified in terms of promising practices. They demonstrate how providers – information seekers – manage, structure and organize the joint problem-solving process. Looking at how they elicit high levels of sticky information (von Hippel, 1994), the four promising practices identified show in-depth how the joint problem-solving process is organized. While one focus is on the provider's view, another focus of this dissertation

[36] Brackets adopted by the original source by Simon (1978).

is the customer in joint problem solving. This complements the analysis of the dyadic problem solving. The better understanding of the customer value in co-creation allows for better designing the problem-solving process along customers' preferences. Further, the two empirical studies shed light on how the joint problem solving can be better designed. For instance, the findings allow for better bridging information asymmetries in high-tech product co-creation, which is found very challenging (Aarikka-Stenroos & Jaakkola, 2012; Nordin & Kowalkowski, 2010; Ulrich & Eppinger, 2012, p. 34; von Hippel, 1994). The organization of joint problem solving is one major challenge in the problem-solving literature, particularly with regard to efficiency and efficacy (Nickerson & Zenger, 2004).

The second contribution relates to sticky information within the problem-solving perspective. As shown in the literature, close and direct customer-provider interactions are most suitable to transfer high levels of sticky information (Ganesan et al., 2005; Mahr et al., 2014). Co-creation is one particularly close interaction that serves to elicit sticky information (Nordin & Kowalkowski, 2010; O'hern & Rindfleisch, 2010). In this regard, it is argued that this dissertation contributes rich insight into the elicitation of sticky information in the context of high-tech product co-creation. Particularly with *Part II* and *Part III,* the topic of sticky information is addressed. On the one hand, the promising practices unmasked showcase how a provider of high-tech products *"generate[s] knowledge that the firm seeks"* (Nickerson & Zenger, 2004, p. 618) by properly organizing the overall co-creation process. Then, with *Part III,* it is argued that the better understanding of the customer value in co-creation enhances the elicitation of sticky information. This is because the customer engagement and motivation can be enhanced, both being decisive in co-creation (Roberts et al., 2014).

The third contribution is the integral view on joint problem solving to co-create high-tech products: the three empirical studies consider all phases of the joint problem-solving process, starting with the earliest phase – supported by a toolkit – and then moving to the face-to-face co-creation of high-tech products. In this vein, it is dealt with different levels of sticky information (Ogawa, 1998; von Hippel, 1994). While two studies tackle the face-to-face process with its high levels of sticky information, one study focuses on how to capture lower levels of sticky information. All results are gathered from both the customer and provider perspective in the dyadic problem solving.

3 Avenues for further research

This dissertation offers fruitful topics for future research. Sure, it is advised to address the qualitative findings with quantitative approaches for their validity on larger scales. Especially regarding the different customer types, it is of strong interest whether these findings apply to other business customers and to other industries.

In this research, each empirical study includes an individual *section* for future research when concluding the parts. Nonetheless, there are also overall avenues for future research, as the author encountered two specifically promising avenues for academic undertakings. These avenues are drawn from his daily work with high-tech SMEs and briefly delineated.

3.1 Toward a DART model for B2B co-creation

As companies must develop co-creation capabilities for co-creating high-tech products (Madhavaram & Appan, 2010), the question arises what tools are appropriate to solve this task. Several recent studies from innovation research call for tools that enable effective co-creation (Barczak, 2012; Gemser & Perks, 2015). One tool to manage co-creation is suggested by Prahalad and Ramaswamy (2004b): the DART model. DART is an acronym, standing for *dialogue, access, reflexivity* and *transparency. Dialogue* relates to promoting proper communication and knowledge sharing, while *access* means that participants can not only use, but modify the co-creation content. *Reflexivity* fosters learning in the sense that the interactions are used to improve the co-creation content as well as the overall experience. Last, *transparency* aims to establish trust. To date, the DART model has not been applied in the B2B context, but recent studies state that the building blocks of DART are a powerful management tool that is heavily overlooked (Taghizadeh, Jayaraman, Ismail, & Rahman, 2016). Being simple and comprehensive (Albinsson, Perera, & Sautter, 2015), the DART model provides a framework that takes the non-linearity of co-creation processes into consideration with its four dimensions.

Only few studies have exploited the richness of the DART model (Solakis, Peña-Vinces, & Lopéz-Bonilla, 2017). One avenue for further research is to map findings of this research, e. g., the promising practices found in *Part II,* on the four dimensions of the DART model. A first mapping of some findings is illustrated in *Figure 24.*

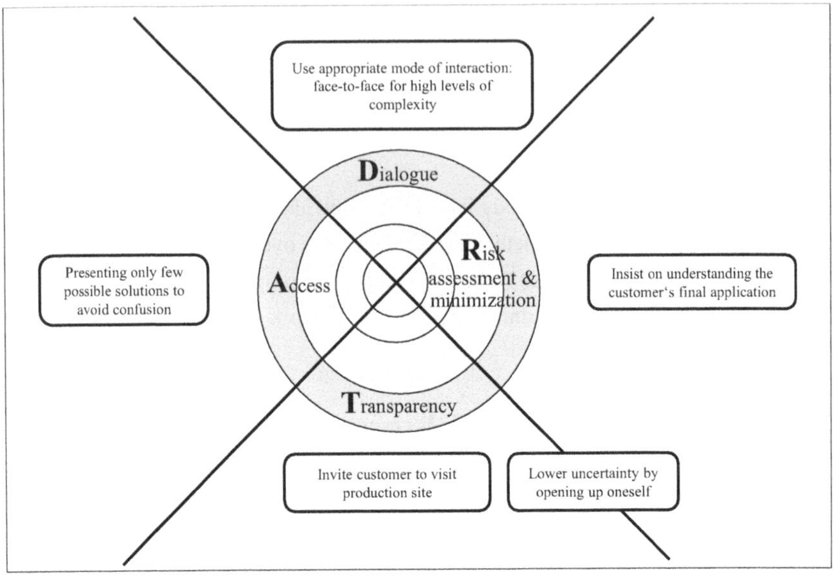

Figure 24: DART model for B2B co-creation[37]

A few suggestions are made in the graphical illustration to detail the avenue for further research. The allocation is done twofold: first, the suggestions are derived from the findings of the dissertation, e. g. *use appropriate mode of interaction*, or *insisting on understanding the customer's final use*. For instance, borderline cases can be mapped on two dimensions, such as *lower uncertainty by opening up oneself.* Second, *presenting only few possible solutions to avoid confusion* is based on extant research (Piller et al., 2005). Here, qualitative research appears suitable to explain its usefulness, perhaps following DSR informed by Peffers and Tuunanen (2007).

[37] Own illustration.

3.2 Designing a B2B toolkit for design-oriented customers

This dissertation delivers strong evidence that, indeed, several business customers wish emotional and social value components within the co-creation process for high-tech products. So far, extant studies on toolkits and configurators in the B2B domain have followed the credo that business customers particularly prefer functional value (Eggert & Ulaga, 2002) – i. e. toolkits exhibit a functionally-driven design. On the one hand side, extant approaches seem appropriate when looking at customers that mainly look for firm criteria. On the other hand side, it is unlikely to properly engage design-oriented customers with a purely functional design. Therefore, it seems promising to integrate the findings of this dissertation of social and emotional value components into a B2B toolkit design. This approach is fueled by the fact that B2B toolkits are considered to *"allow real innovation"* (Franke & Piller, 2004, p. 405). With the findings, more playful toolkit designs can be informed also for B2B research. Nuanced insight in how to design according toolkits is, e. g., provided in the mass customization literature. The latter has been heavily concerned with toolkit design for addressing the customer desire of enjoyment, creativity or pride-of-authorship (Fogliatto et al., 2012; Franke et al., 2010; Merle et al., 2010).

4 Managerial implications: six questions answered

Several voices state that the topic of co-creation lacks knowledge for practical application (e. g. Frow et al., 2015; Mustak et al., 2013). It is argued that the findings of this research entail useful knowledge for managers.

Three questions are answered to summarize the empirical studies for managers very briefly. Looking at the sequence, it makes sense to start with the managerial implication from the third study of *Part IV* as this relates to the preparation before the actual face-to-face co-creation. Implications from the other empirical parts are arranged on the right hand side, illustrated in *Figure 25*:

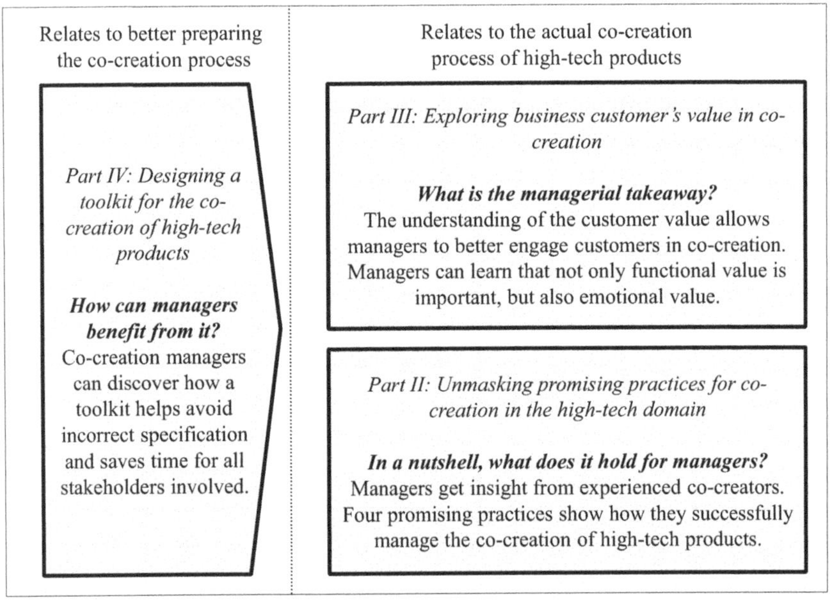

Figure 25: Three questions answered for managers from each empirical study

After summarizing the studies for managers, the focus is on the three managerial challenges[38] related to the co-creation of high-tech products in B2B. These challenges are *time intensity*, *requirement capturing*, and *customer engagement*, provided in *Figure 26, Figure 27,* and *Figure 28* with related questions and answers for managers. These implications are derived across the empirical studies.

Challenge related to *time intensity*:
Managers struggle with the efficiency of the co-creation of high-tech products.

Leading to the question:
How can managers save time with regard to co-creating high-tech products?

Saving time in the early stage with a toolkit

- Appropriate toolkit functions enable managers to better assess customer's purchase intention. Ideally, this serves to sort out some requests earlier.
- Gathering information with a toolkit on the final use of the product and other requirements allows managers to better prepare the face-to-face co-creation. This has the potential to drastically save time, as this can replace some early face-to-face meetings.
- Other toolkit functions permit to eliminate some customer requests early, which makes further interaction unnecessary in some cases.

Saving time in the face-to-face interaction

- When managers succeed to build an open and trustful relationship, customers are more likely to open up themselves. This saves time as they share information faster.
- For quickly reaching shared understanding, it makes sense to use boundary objects such as prototypes or other tangibles to explain product details.
- Especially with efficiency-driven customers there is large potential to save time in co-creation projects. However, managers need to ensure that they deliver the required input, as these customers often tend to show unwillingness for co-creation.
- Looking at design-oriented customers, it is useful to acknowledge that there are no great potentials for time saving, because these customers wish for time-intense and playful co-creation processes.
- Managers are advised to organize "co-creation hackathons", as this allows best to focus the most relevant tasks on one single day.
- For faster decision-making, co-creation managers should involve customers' customers and decision-makers in, for instance, the "co-creation hackathons".

Figure 26: Question answered for managers facing the challenge *time intensity*

[38] This dissertation picks up three challenges for providers in its *Part II*. For an overview of related literature, see *2.1 Underlying challenges: Co-creating high-tech products.*

Challenge related to *requirement capturing*:
Managers often fail to capture customers' requirements properly.

Leading to the question:
How can managers avoid incorrect specification in the co-creation of high-tech products?

Avoiding incorrect specification in the early stage with a toolkit
- Toolkits that collect information on the final are useful for managers as they allow concluding a series of requirements.
- Toolkits are powerful to eliminate unfeasible combinations of properties very early.

Avoiding incorrect specification in the face-to-face interaction
- Managers are advised to demonstrate customers that knowing the final use is decisive to successfully co-create the product.
- It makes sense for managers to insist on understanding the final use of the product. In the event that customers refuse to reveal that, this can entail an abortion of the co-creation.
- It is helpful to enable customers intensively. As they know their own business better, this can empower them to also discover incorrect specification.
- When managers adapt co-creation processes along customers' preferences, customers are more likely to make valuable contributions. This improves the requirement capturing.

Figure 27: Question answered for managers facing the challenge *requirement capturing*

Challenge related to *customer engagement*:
Managers face problems to engage business customers into the co-creation of high-tech products.

Leading to the question:
How can managers better involve customers along their preferences?

Better involving customers into the early stage with a toolkit
- For all points concerning the toolkit, it is decisive for managers to understand that the requested information is not too complex. Otherwise, the customer cannot articulate it.

Better involving customers into the face-to-face interaction
- Customer preferences in the co-creation process are diverse: customers are between the poles of being design-oriented or efficiency-driven. They need to be involved in very different ways.
- For design-oriented customers, managers are recommended to design time-intensive, playful co-creation processes in order to benefit from motivated participants and valuable contributions. In total: increase interaction with this customer type.
- For efficiency-driven customers, it is advised to stress their important contribution to a successful co-creation. In total: decrease interaction with this customer type and take as many tasks of their shoulders.

Figure 28: Question answered for managers facing the challenge *customer engagement*

5 Concluding remarks

5.1 Limitations

The dissertation at hand is not without limitations. This *section* depicts the limitations of this research. As each part of the empirical studies in *Part II, Part III* and *Part IV* contains an individual limitation, the following paragraphs depict the limitations on an overarching level. The limitations of this research are twofold, referring to industry peculiarities and the qualitative research approach.

Starting with the industry peculiarities, this limitation touches upon the domain of the context in which the research at hand was conducted. This limitation concerns two points regarding the SME focus in the German textile industry and one specific peculiarity in this domain. First, for the SME context, it must be acknowledged that all empirical studies have been carried out in niche-specialized companies that are – as one unique selling point – already characterized by strong customer orientation and closeness (Teirlinck & Spithoven, 2013; Usman et al., 2018). Therefore, the implementation of open innovation methods such as co-creation has not yielded fundamental restructuration to them. As shown in the studies, there are typically only few persons concerned with co-creation. It appears easier to implement a novel approach with only few persons then one or several entire departments. This is why large corporations are likely to encounter more challenges than SMEs when implementing co-creation. However, this limitation is considered as strength, when turning the viewpoint: this industry is particularly interesting and appropriate, as they have worked for decades on integrating customers into their innovation activities. Rather informal practices have been developed and approved. The findings drawn from this SME context are considered fruitful and relevant also for large corporations, as recent studies stress (Teirlinck, 2018; Usman et al., 2018). As a consequence, the SME focus is considered as both a limitation and strength of this research. The second point highlights a theme that was found throughout the entire database, namely the importance of boundary objects in the textile industry. Although there are numerous key figures for textiles, for instance describing the flowing fall of a textile, still there is the irrevocable wish by the customer to feel, touch and see the textile in real-life. Hence, within the textile industry, samples or tangibles are important due to multisensory experiences. The limitation stems from the assumption that such experiences are unlikely to be translatable to other industries such as machinery. Nonetheless, high-tech product characteristics are part of numerous other domains, where intense face-to-face interaction is needed. As a consequence, these are, arguably, synonymous for many other facets that are difficult to articulate.

Looking at the qualitative research approach, the findings of this dissertation are also to some extent limited. A closer look appears requisite because the qualitative approach is often critiqued for lacking scholarly rigor despite of its popularity in management research (Gioia et al., 2013). Although the empirical studies added rather deep insights to this field, the findings remain descriptive, especially regarding *Part II* and *Part III*. However, the major goal was not to achieve breadth, but rather in-depth insights in this exploration phase. Another point is that, although the sizes of sample are rich for qualitative research (Fusch & Ness, 2015), and although a comparably large number of companies contributed, the findings are based on interviews as well as focus group data conducted with actors involved in co-creation from the provider and customer perspective, which poses a limitation. This is because the findings rely on the validity of this data. In particular, the author was not given the chance to evaluate the findings of the empirical studies in real-life settings. For that, the shadowing technique would be particularly useful. Or, for instance, longitudinal approaches would boost the value of this research, exploiting the rich potentials lying in qualitative research. Nonetheless, the interview and focus group approach within the numerous company visits permitted to elicit a better understanding of the dynamic development of current practices. This would have been unexplored with an ethnographic approach such as the shadowing technique.

5.2 Final notes

To conclude, this dissertation investigated an increasingly important topic in research and practice alike. It focused on examining the phenomenon of the co-creation of high-tech products in the B2B domain. It put special emphasis on a better understanding of current practices and detailed activities. From different angles, the topic under investigation was approached. Based on a strong engagement of the researcher, the dissertation was carried out by involving numerous companies from the German textile industry. Three research gaps in extant literature were detected and sought to be addressed with three empirical studies – all relevant for both research and practice.

Besides the described contributions to research, I take the liberty to conclude this work with personal thoughts on the practical usefulness of the findings. As already mentioned, I have been working with the German textile industry rather extensively during the last years. As my core topic, I addressed the research of this dissertation in a large-scale research initiative, leading two co-creation projects within this context. As a consequence, the results were communicated on numerous occasions to practitioners, including both presentations in front of dozens of industry representatives and one-to-one collaborations. Typically, the feedback was coined by the credo that the findings – especially the different customer types – are particularly helpful to reflect current business practices. Although the practitioners already had *knowledge* about such different customer types, this had to be labeled, scientifically structured and brought to their attention to translate it into according actions for their businesses. Especially, I perceived that the practitioners greatly acknowledged to get structured, sometimes rather abstract insights into their own business from an external person without any reservation. Into the bargain, the abstraction directly impacted several cases – this has at least come to my knowledge in a handful of cases – to realign existing structures. For instance, for one company some of the results of this research were used, with only little adaptation, to formulate the requirements for a toolkit in an intricate medical application. Moreover, eventually, the toolkit design presented in *Part III* has been introduced in the focal company and integrated in the existing IT landscape. Having seen that in real-life, I beg to say that I have seen parts of my research results in practical application, which makes me delighted as an engaged researcher. More precisely, the artefact developed in *Part*

IV represents an integral part of a large digital transformation project within the focal company that focuses on rethinking the entire customer interaction.

Last but not least, I am looking forward to pushing further the communication of my research for the academic community. Parts of it have already been presented to academic conferences[39], especially to innovation researchers. Now, I am excited to share the findings of this dissertation also with researchers from related domains, as co-creation is one highly interdisciplinary field. In particular, I am looking forward to bringing the topic of emotional and social value closer to B2B research – because this comes with major consequences in manifold regards and has been widely neglected.

[39] All publications of this dissertation's author are listed in *Annex I*.

References

L. K. Grafmüller, *Co-Creation of High-Tech Products in the B2B Domain*,
Markt- und Unternehmensentwicklung Markets and Organisations,
https://doi.org/10.1007/978-3-658-28412-1

Aarikka-Stenroos, L., & Jaakkola, E. (2012). Value co-creation in knowledge intensive business services: A dyadic perspective on the joint problem solving process. *Industrial Marketing Management*, *41*(1), 15–26. https://doi.org/10.1016/j.indmarman.2011.11.008

Achilladelis, B., Jervis, P., & Robertson, A. (1971). A Study of Success and Failure in Industrial Innovation: Report on Project SAPPHO to SRC. University of Sussex.

Adler, U. (2004). Structural change: The dominant feature in the economic development of the German textile and clothing industries. *Journal of Fashion Marketing and Management: an International Journal*, *8*(3), 300–319. https://doi.org/10.1108/13612020410547815

Alam, I. (2006). Removing the fuzziness from the fuzzy front-end of service innovations through customer interactions. *Industrial Marketing Management*, *35*(4), 468–480. https://doi.org/10.1016/j.indmarman.2005.04.004

Albinsson, P. A., Perera, B. Y., & Sautter, P. T. (2015). DART Scale Development: Diagnosing a Firm's Readiness for Strategic Value Co-creation. *Journal of Marketing Theory and Practice*, *24*(1), 42–58. https://doi.org/10.1080/10696679.2016.1089763

Alejandro, T. B., Souza, D. V., Boles, J. S., Ribeiro, Á. H. P., & Monteiro, P. R. R. (2011). The outcome of company and account manager relationship quality on loyalty, relationship value and performance. *Industrial Marketing Management*, *40*(1), 36–43. https://doi.org/10.1016/j.indmarman.2010.09.008

Anderson, J. C., & Narus, J. A. (1998). Business marketing: Understand what customers value. *Harvard Business Review*, *76*(6), 53.

Anderson, J. C., & Wynstra, F. (2010). Purchasing Higher-Value, Higher-Price Offerings in Business Markets. *Journal of Business-to-Business Marketing*, *17*(1), 29–61. https://doi.org/10.1080/10517120903000363

Anderson, R. E. (1996). Personal selling and sales management in the new millennium. *Journal of Personal Selling & Sales Management*, *16*(4), 17–32.

Arslanagic-Kalajdzic, M., & Zabkar, V. (2017). Is perceived value more than value for money in professional business services? *Industrial Marketing Management*, *65*, 47–58. https://doi.org/10.1016/j.indmarman.2017.05.005

Backman, M., Börjesson, S., & Setterberg, S. (2007). Working with concepts in the fuzzy front end: Exploring the context for innovation for different types of concepts at Volvo Cars. *R&D Management*, *37*(1). https://doi.org/10.1111/j.1467-9310.2007.00455.x

Ballantyne, D., & Varey, R. J. (2006). Creating value-in-use through marketing interaction: The exchange logic of relating, communicating and knowing. *Marketing Theory*, *6*(3), 335–348. https://doi.org/10.1177/1470593106066795

Barczak, G. (2012). The Future of NPD/Innovation Research. *Journal of Product Innovation Management*, *29*(3), 355–357. https://doi.org/10.1111/j.1540-5885.2012.00907.x

Bare, M., & Cox, J. J. (2008). Applying principles of mass customization to improve the empirical product development process. *Journal of Intelligent Manufacturing*, *19*(5), 565–576. https://doi.org/10.1007/s10845-008-0134-0

Barley, S. R., & Kunda, G. (2001). Bringing Work Back In. *Organization Science*, *12*(1), 76–95. https://doi.org/10.1287/orsc.12.1.76.10122

Baumann, J., & Le Meunier-FitzHugh, K. (2014). Making value co-creation a reality – exploring the co-creative value processes in customer–salesperson interaction. *Journal of Marketing Management*, *31*(3-4), 289–316. https://doi.org/10.1080/0267257X.2014.956137

Beer, S. (2001). Branchenskizze: Ostdeutsche Textilindustrie. *Wirtschaft Im Wandel*, *7*(9), 216–217.

Bessant, J., Kaplinsky, R., & Lamming, R. (2003). Putting supply chain learning into practice. *International Journal of Operations & Production Management*, *23*(2), 167–184. https://doi.org/10.1108/01443570310458438

Bettencourt, L. A., Ostrom, A. L., Brown, S. W., & Roundtree, R. I. (2002). Client Co-Production in Knowledge-Intensive Business Services. *California Management Review*, *44*(4), 100–128. https://doi.org/10.2307/41166145

Beutel, T., Jonas, J. M., & Möslein, K. M. (2017). Co-Creation and User Involvement in a Living Lab: An Evaluation of Applied Methods. In J. M. Leimeister & W. Brenner (Eds.), *Proceedings der 13. Internationalen Tagung Wirtschaftsinformatik (WI 2017)* (pp. 1453–1464). St. Gallen.

Biemans, W., & Langerak, F. (2015). More Research Priorities. *Journal of Product Innovation Management*, *32*(1), 2–3. https://doi.org/10.1111/jpim.12255

Bogers, M., Afuah, A., & Bastian, B. (2010). Users as Innovators: A Review, Critique, and Future Research Directions. *Journal of Management*, *36*(4), 857–875. https://doi.org/10.1177/0149206309353944

Brun, E., Steinar Saetre, A., & Gjelsvik, M. (2009). Classification of ambiguity in new product development projects. *European Journal of Innovation Management*, *12*(1), 62–85. https://doi.org/10.1108/14601060910928175

Bstieler, L., Gruen, T., Akdeniz, B., Brick, D., Du, S., & Guo, L. (2018). Emerging Research Themes in Innovation and New Product Development: Insights from the 2017 PDMA-UNH Doctoral Consortium. *Journal of Product Innovation Management*, *35*(3), 300–307. https://doi.org/10.1111/jpim.12447

Candi, M., & Kahn, K. B. (2016). Functional, emotional, and social benefits of new B2B services. *Industrial Marketing Management*, *57*, 177–184. https://doi.org/10.1016/j.indmarman.2016.02.002

Carlile, P. R. (2002). A Pragmatic View of Knowledge and Boundaries: Boundary Objects in New Product Development. *Organization Science*, *13*(4), 442–455. https://doi.org/10.1287/orsc.13.4.442.2953

Cho, H.-J., & Pucik, V. (2005). Relationship between innovativeness, quality, growth, profitability, and market value. *Strategic Management Journal*, *26*(6), 555–575. https://doi.org/10.1002/smj.461

Clarke, I., & Flaherty, T. B. (2003). Web-based B2B portals. *Industrial Marketing Management*, *32*(1), 15–23. https://doi.org/10.1016/S0019-8501(01)00199-7

Conner, K. R. (1991). A Historical Comparison of Resource-Based Theory and Five Schools of Thought Within Industrial Organization Economics: Do We Have a New Theory of the Firm? *Journal of Management, 17*(1), 121–154. https://doi.org/10.1177/014920639101700109

Cooper, R. (1999). From Experience The invisible success factors in product innovation. *Journal of Product Innovation Management, 16*(2), 115–133. https://doi.org/10.1016/S0737-6782(98)00061-7

Cooper, R., & Kleinschmidt, E. J. (1986). An investigation into the new product process: Steps, deficiencies, and impact. *Journal of Product Innovation Management, 3*(2), 71–85. https://doi.org/10.1016/0737-6782(86)90030-5

Cooper, R. G. (2008). *Winning at new products: Accelerating the process from idea to launch* (3. ed, repr). New York: Basic Books.

Corbin, J. M., & Strauss, A. L. (2008). *Basics of qualitative research: Techniques and procedures for developing grounded theory* (3. ed.). Los Angeles, Calif.: Sage Publ.

Cross, N. (Ed.). (1972). *Design participation. Proceedings of the Design Research Society's Conference on Design Participation, held in Manchester, Sept. 1971*. London: Academy Ed.

Cui, A. S., & Wu, F. (2017). The Impact of Customer Involvement on New Product Development: Contingent and Substitutive Effects. *Journal of Product Innovation Management, 34*(1), 60–80. https://doi.org/10.1111/jpim.12326

Daft, R. L., & Lengel, R. H. (1986). Organizational Information Requirements, Media Richness and Structural Design. *Management Science, 32*(5), 554–571. https://doi.org/10.1287/mnsc.32.5.554

Davies, A., Brady, T., & Hobday, M. (2007). Organizing for solutions: Systems seller vs. systems integrator. *Industrial Marketing Management, 36*(2), 183–193. https://doi.org/10.1016/j.indmarman.2006.04.009

Dennis, A. R., & Valacich, J. S. (1999). Rethinking Media Richness: Towards a Theory of Media Synchronicity. *Proceedings of the 32nd Hawaii International Conference on System Sciences.*

Dolez, P. I., & Vu-Khanh, T. (2009). Recent Developments and Needs in Materials Used for Personal Protective Equipment and Their Testing. *International Journal of Occupational Safety and Ergonomics, 15*(4), 347–362.

Drucker, P. F. (1954). *The practice of management* (1. ed.). New York: Harper.

Ebnet, M. (2014). Branche im Blickpunkt: Das Textil- und Bekleidungsgewerbe in Europa und Deutschland – Totgesagte leben länger. *Ifo Schnelldienst, 67*(5), 35–40.

Eggert, A., & Ulaga, W. (2002). Customer perceived value: A substitute for satisfaction in business markets? *Journal of Business & Industrial Marketing, 17*(2/3), 107–118. https://doi.org/10.1108/08858620210419754

Eggert, A., Ulaga, W., & Schultz, F. (2006). Value creation in the relationship life cycle: A quasi-longitudinal analysis. *Industrial Marketing Management, 35*(1), 20–27. https://doi.org/10.1016/j.indmarman.2005.07.003

Eisenhardt, K. M. (1989). Building Theories from Case Study Research. *Academy of Management Review, 14*(4), 532–550. https://doi.org/10.5465/AMR.1989.4308385

Engelbrektsson, P., & Söderman, M. (2004). The use and perception of methods and product representations in product development: A survey of Swedish industry. *Journal of Engineering Design, 15*(2), 141–154. https://doi.org/10.1080/09544820310001641245

Enkel, E., Kausch, C., & Gassmann, O. (2005). Managing the Risk of Customer Integration. *European Management Journal, 23*(2), 203–213. https://doi.org/10.1016/j.emj.2005.02.005

Fang, E., Palmatier, R. W., & Evans, K. R. (2008). Influence of customer participation on creating and sharing of new product value. *Journal of the Academy of Marketing Science, 36*(3), 322–336. https://doi.org/10.1007/s11747-007-0082-9

Fauska, P., Kryvinska, N., & Strauss, C. (2014). Agile Management of Complex Goods & Services Bundles for B2B E-Commerce by Global Narrow-Specialized Companies. *Global Journal of Flexible Systems Management, 15*(1), 5–23. https://doi.org/10.1007/s40171-013-0054-5

Felin, T., & Zenger, T. R. (2014). Closed or open innovation? Problem solving and the governance choice. *Research Policy, 43*(5), 914–925. https://doi.org/10.1016/j.respol.2013.09.006

Fischer, A. (2003). *Analyse veränderter Tätigkeitsinhalte, Arbeits-und Leistungsbedingungen in der sächsischen Textilindustrie.*

Flanagan, J. C. (1954). The critical incident technique. *Psychological Bulletin, 51*(4), 327–358. https://doi.org/10.1037/h0061470

Flint, D. J., Woodruff, R. B., & Gardial, S. F. (1997). Customer value change in industrial marketing relationships: A call for new strategies and research. *Industrial Marketing Management, 26*(2), 163–175. https://doi.org/10.1016/S0019-8501(96)00112-5

Fogliatto, F. S., Da Silveira, G., & Borenstein, D. (2012). The mass customization decade: An updated review of the literature. *International Journal of Production Economics, 138*(1), 14–25. https://doi.org/10.1016/j.ijpe.2012.03.002

Forza, C., & Salvador, F. (2007). *Product information management for mass customization: Connecting customer, front-office, and back-office for fast and efficient customization.* Basingstoke, Hampshire: Palgrave Macmillan. Retrieved from http://www.palgraveconnect.com/pc/doifinder/10.1057/9780230800922

Foss, N. J. (1996). Knowledge-Based Approaches to the Theory of the Firm: Some Critical Comments. *Organization Science, 7*(5), 470–476. https://doi.org/10.1287/orsc.7.5.470

Franke, N., & Piller, F. (2003). Key research issues in user interaction with user toolkits in a mass customisation system. *International Journal of Technology Management, 26*(5/6), 578. https://doi.org/10.1504/IJTM.2003.003424

Franke, N., & Piller, F. (2004). Value Creation by Toolkits for User Innovation and Design: The Case of the Watch Market. *Journal of Product Innovation Management, 21*(6), 401–415. https://doi.org/10.1111/j.0737-6782.2004.00094.x

Franke, N., Schreier, M., & Kaiser, U. (2010). The "I Designed It Myself" Effect in Mass Customization. *Management Science, 56*(1), 125–140. https://doi.org/10.1287/mnsc.1090.1077

Frow, P., Nenonen, S., Payne, A., & Storbacka, K. (2015). Managing Co-creation Design: A Strategic Approach to Innovation. *British Journal of Management*. Advance online publication. https://doi.org/10.1111/1467-8551.12087

Füller, J., Faullant, R., & Matzler, K. (2010). Triggers for virtual customer integration in the development of medical equipment — From a manufacturer and a user's perspective. *Industrial Marketing Management*, *39*(8), 1376–1383. https://doi.org/10.1016/j.indmarman.2010.04.003

Füller, J., Hutter, K., & Faullant, R. (2011). Why co-creation experience matters? Creative experience and its impact on the quantity and quality of creative contributions. *R&D Management*, *41*(3), 259–273. https://doi.org/10.1111/j.1467-9310.2011.00640.x

Fusch, P. I., & Ness, L. R. (2015). Are We There Yet? Data Saturation in Qualitative Research. *Qualitative Report*, *20*(9), 1408–1416.

Galvagno, M., & Dalli, D. (2014). Theory of value co-creation: A systematic literature review. *Managing Service Quality: an International Journal*, *24*(6), 643–683. https://doi.org/10.1108/MSQ-09-2013-0187

Gambardella, A., Raasch, C., & von Hippel, E. (2017). The User Innovation Paradigm: Impacts on Markets and Welfare. *Management Science*, *63*(5), 1450–1468. https://doi.org/10.1287/mnsc.2015.2393

Ganesan, S., Malter, A. J., & Rindfleisch, A. (2005). Does Distance Still Matter? Geographic Proximity and New Product Development. *Journal of Marketing*, *69*(4), 44–60. https://doi.org/10.1509/jmkg.2005.69.4.44

Gebhardt, R., Barteld, M., Grafmüller, L., Mosig, T., & Weiß, M. (2017). Mass Customized Technical Textiles in the B2B Sector. *IOP Conference Series: Materials Science and Engineering*, *254*, 152004. https://doi.org/10.1088/1757-899X/254/15/152004

Gemser, G., & Perks, H. (2015). Co-Creation with Customers: An Evolving Innovation Research Field. *Journal of Product Innovation Management*, *32*(5), 660–665. https://doi.org/10.1111/jpim.12279

Gesamtverband textil+mode. (2017). *Die deutsche Textil- und Modeindustrie in Zahlen.*

Geyer, F., Lehnen, J., & Herstatt, C. (2018). Customer Need Identification Methods in New Product Development: What Works "Best"? *International Journal of Innovation and Technology Management*, *15*(01), 1850008. https://doi.org/10.1142/S0219877018500086

Ghosh, M., Dutta, S., & Stremersch, S. (2006). Customizing Complex Products: When Should the Vendor Take Control? *Journal of Marketing Research*, *43*(4), 664–679. https://doi.org/10.1509/jmkr.43.4.664

Gilmore, J. H., & Pine, B. J. (1997). The four faces of mass customization. *Harvard Business Review*, *75*(1), 91–101.

Gil-Saura, I., Frasquet-Deltoro, M., & Cervera-Taulet, A. (2009). The value of B2B relationships. *Industrial Management & Data Systems*, *109*(5), 593–609. https://doi.org/10.1108/02635570910957605

Gioia, D. A., Corley, K. G., & Hamilton, A. L. (2013). Seeking Qualitative Rigor in Inductive Research. *Organizational Research Methods, 16*(1), 15–31. https://doi.org/10.1177/1094428112452151

Glaser, B. G. (1965). The Constant Comparative Method of Qualitative Analysis. *Social Problems, 12*(4), 436–445. https://doi.org/10.2307/798843

Gordon, G. L., Calantone, R. J., & Di Benedetto, C. A. (1993). Business-to-business Service Marketing: How does it differ from Business-to-business Product Marketing? *Journal of Business & Industrial Marketing, 8*(1), 45–57. https://doi.org/10.1108/08858629310027605

Gosling, J., & Naim, M. M. (2009). Engineer-to-order supply chain management: A literature review and research agenda. *International Journal of Production Economics, 122*(2), 741–754. https://doi.org/10.1016/j.ijpe.2009.07.002

Graevenitz, G. von, Wagner, S., & Harhoff, D. (2011). How to measure patent thickets? A novel approach. *Economics Letters, 111*(1), 6–9. https://doi.org/10.1016/j.econlet.2010.12.005

Grafmüller, L. K., Hankammer, S., Hönigsberg, S., & Wache, H. (2018). Developing complex, mass-customized products in SME networks: Perspectives from co-creation, solution space development, and information system design. *International Journal of Industrial Engineering and Management, 9*(4), 215-227.

Grafmüller, L. K., & Möslein, K. M. (2017). Customer Co-Creation – Wie aus Kundenwünschen interaktiv ein Produktdesign entsteht. In H.-H. Jung & P. Kraft (Eds.), *Digital vernetzt. Transformation der Wertschöpfung: Szenarien, Optionen und Erfolgsmodelle für smarte Geschäftsmodelle, Produkte und Services* (pp. 57–70). München: Hanser.

Grant, R. M. (1996). Toward a knowledge-based theory of the firm. *Strategic Management Journal, 17*(S2), 109–122.

Grönroos, C. (2004). The relationship marketing process: Communication, interaction, dialogue, value. *Journal of Business & Industrial Marketing, 19*(2), 99–113. https://doi.org/10.1108/08858620410523981

Grönroos, C., & Ravald, A. (2011). Service as business logic: Implications for value creation and marketing. *Journal of Service Management, 22*(1), 5–22. https://doi.org/10.1108/09564231111106893

Grönroos, C., & Voima, P. (2013). Critical service logic: Making sense of value creation and co-creation. *Journal of the Academy of Marketing Science, 41*(2), 133–150. https://doi.org/10.1007/s11747-012-0308-3

Haas, A., Snehota, I., & Corsaro, D. (2012). Creating value in business relationships: The role of sales. *Industrial Marketing Management, 41*(1), 94–105. https://doi.org/10.1016/j.indmarman.2011.11.004

Hakanen, T., & Jaakkola, E. (2012). Co-creating customer-focused solutions within business networks: A service perspective. *Journal of Service Management, 23*(4), 593–611. https://doi.org/10.1108/09564231211260431

Haller, J. B. A., Bullinger, A. C., & Möslein, K. M. (2011). Innovationswettbewerbe. *WIRTSCHAFTSINFORMATIK*, *53*(2), 105–108. https://doi.org/10.1007/s11576-011-0262-6

Harmancioglu, N., McNally, R. C., Calantone, R. J., & Durmusoglu, S. S. (2007). Your new product development (NPD) is only as good as your process: An exploratory analysis of new NPD process design and implementation. *R&D Management*, *37*(5), 399–424. https://doi.org/10.1111/j.1467-9310.2007.00486.x

Harrison, G. W., & List, J. A. (2004). Field experiments. *Journal of Economic Literature*, *42*(3), 1009–1055.

Haug, A., Hvam, L., & Mortensen, N. H. (2013). Reducing variety in product solution spaces of engineer-to-order companies: The case of Novenco A/S. *International Journal of Product Development*, *18*(6), 531. https://doi.org/10.1504/IJPD.2013.058556

Haug, A., Ladeby, K., & Edwards, K. (2009). From engineer-to-order to mass customization. *Management Research News*, *32*(7), 633–644. https://doi.org/10.1108/01409170910965233

Hawkins, T. G., Gravier, M. J., Berkowitz, D., & Muir, W. A. (2015). Improving services supply management in the defense sector: How the procurement process affects B2B service quality. *Journal of Purchasing and Supply Management*, *21*(2), 81–94. https://doi.org/10.1016/j.pursup.2014.12.007

Heide, J. B., & John, G. (1990). Alliances in Industrial Purchasing: The Determinants of Joint Action in Buyer-Supplier Relationships. *Journal of Marketing Research*, *27*(1), 24. https://doi.org/10.2307/3172548

Hemetsberger, A., & Godula, G. (2007). Virtual Customer Integration in New Product Development in Industrial Markets: The QLL Framework. *Journal of Business-to-Business Marketing*, *14*(2), 1–40. https://doi.org/10.1300/J033v14n02_01

Hevner, A. R., March, S. T., Park, J., & Ram, S. (2004). Design science in information systems research. *MIS Quarterly*, *28*(1), 75–105.

Hicks, C., McGovern, T., & Earl, C. (2000). Supply chain management: A strategic issue in engineer to order manufacturing. *International Journal of Production Economics*, *65*(2), 179–190. https://doi.org/10.1016/S0925-5273(99)00026-2

Hienerth, C., & Lettl, C. (2011). Exploring How Peer Communities Enable Lead User Innovations to Become Standard Equipment in the Industry: Community Pull Effects. *Journal of Product Innovation Management*, *28*(s1), 175–195. https://doi.org/10.1111/j.1540-5885.2011.00869.x

Hobday, M. (1998). Product complexity, innovation and industrial organisation. *Research Policy*, *26*(6), 689–710. https://doi.org/10.1016/S0048-7333(97)00044-9

Hobday, M., & Rush, H. (1999). Technology management in complex product systems (CoPS) - ten questions answered. *International Journal of Technology Management*, *17*(6), 618. https://doi.org/10.1504/IJTM.1999.002739

Hochleitner, F. P., Arbussà, A., & Coenders, G. (2016). Inbound open innovation in SMEs: Indicators, non-financial outcomes and entry-timing. *Technology Analysis & Strategic Management, 29*(2), 204–218. https://doi.org/10.1080/09537325.2016.1211264

Hohenschwert, L., & Geiger, S. (2015). Interpersonal influence strategies in complex B2B sales and the socio-cognitive construction of relationship value. *Industrial Marketing Management, 49*, 139–150. https://doi.org/10.1016/j.indmarman.2015.05.027

Holbrook, M. B. (1994). The nature of customer value: an axiology of services in the consumption experience. In R. T. Rust & R. L. Oliver (Eds.), *Service quality: New directions in theory and practice* (pp. 21–71). Thousand Oaks, Cal.: SAGE.

Howe, J. (2006). The rise of crowdsourcing. *Wired Magazine, 14*(6), 1–4.

Hoyer, W. D., Chandy, R., Dorotic, M., Krafft, M., & Singh, S. S. (2010). Consumer Cocreation in New Product Development. *Journal of Service Research, 13*(3), 283–296. https://doi.org/10.1177/1094670510375604

Huang, S., & Holden, D. (2016). The R&D Boundaries of the Firm: A Problem-Solving Perspective. *International Journal of the Economics of Business, 23*(3), 287–317. https://doi.org/10.1080/13571516.2016.1156247

Huff, A. S. (2009). *Designing research for publication.* Los Angeles: Sage Publ.

Ihl, C., & Piller, F. (2010). Von Kundenorientierung zu Customer Co-Creation im Innovationsprozess. *Marketing Review St. Gallen, 27*(4), 8–13. https://doi.org/10.1007/s11621-010-0071-0

Jaakkola, E., & Alexander, M. (2014). The Role of Customer Engagement Behavior in Value Co-Creation. *Journal of Service Research, 17*(3), 247–261. https://doi.org/10.1177/1094670514529187

Jaakkola, E., & Hakanen, T. (2013). Value co-creation in solution networks. *Industrial Marketing Management, 42*(1), 47–58. https://doi.org/10.1016/j.indmarman.2012.11.005

Jacob, F. (2006). Preparing industrial suppliers for customer integration. *Industrial Marketing Management, 35*(1), 45–56. https://doi.org/10.1016/j.indmarman.2005.08.007

Jacob, F., & Ulaga, W. (2008). The transition from product to service in business markets: An agenda for academic inquiry. *Industrial Marketing Management, 37*(3), 247–253. https://doi.org/10.1016/j.indmarman.2007.09.009

Jeppesen, L. B., & Lakhani, K. R. (2010). Marginality and Problem-Solving Effectiveness in Broadcast Search. *Organization Science, 21*(5), 1016–1033. https://doi.org/10.1287/orsc.1090.0491

Johnsen, T. E., & Ford, D. (2007). Customer approaches to product development with suppliers. *Industrial Marketing Management, 36*(3), 300–308. https://doi.org/10.1016/j.indmarman.2005.09.004

Keinz, P., Hienerth, C., & Lettl, C. (2012). Designing the Organization for User Innovation. *Journal of Organization Design, 1*(3), 20–36.

Kitzinger, J. (1995). Qualitative research. Introducing focus groups. *BMJ: British Medical Journal, 311*(7000), 299–302.

Kleinaltenkamp, M., Bach, T., & Griese, I. (2009). Der Kundenintegrationsbegriff im (Dienstleistungs-) Marketing. In M. Bruhn & B. Stauss (Eds.), *Kundenintegration* (pp. 35–62). Wiesbaden: Gabler. https://doi.org/10.1007/978-3-8349-9407-3_2

Koen, P., Ajamian, G., Burkart, R., Clamen, A., Davidson, J., D'Amore, R., . . . Wagner, K. (2001). Providing Clarity and A Common Language to the "Fuzzy Front End". *Research-Technology Management, 44*(2), 46–55. https://doi.org/10.1080/08956308.2001.11671418

Kohtamäki, M., & Rajala, R. (2016). Theory and practice of value co-creation in B2B systems. *Industrial Marketing Management, 56*, 4–13. https://doi.org/10.1016/j.indmarman.2016.05.027

Kortge, G., & Okonkwo, P. A. (1993). Perceived value approach to pricing. *Industrial Marketing Management, 22*(2), 133–140. https://doi.org/10.1016/0019-8501(93)90039-A

Krippendorf, W., Holst, G., & Richter, U. (2009). *Branchenanalyse Textilindustrie. Untersuchungen zur Situation und Entwicklung der Branchen „Textilgewerbe" (WZ 17). Projektbericht an die Hans Böckler Stiftung. Projekt-Nr. S-2008-201-1.* Düsseldorf.

Kumar, A., & Grisaffe, D. B. (2004). Effects of Extrinsic Attributes on Perceived Quality, Customer Value, and Behavioral Intentions in B2B Settings: A Comparison Across Goods and Service Industries. *Journal of Business-to-Business Marketing, 11*(4), 43–74. https://doi.org/10.1300/J033v11n04_03

La Rocca, A., Moscatelli, P., Perna, A., & Snehota, I. (2016). Customer involvement in new product development in B2B: The role of sales. *Industrial Marketing Management, 58*, 45–57. https://doi.org/10.1016/j.indmarman.2016.05.014

Laage-Hellman, J., Lind, F., & Perna, A. (2014). Customer Involvement in Product Development: An Industrial Network Perspective. *Journal of Business-to-Business Marketing, 21*(4), 257–276. https://doi.org/10.1080/1051712X.2014.979594

Lakhani, K. R., Lifshitz-Assaf, H., & Tushman, M. L. (2013). Open innovation and organizational boundaries: task decomposition, knowledge distribution and the locus of innovation. In A. Grandori (Ed.), *Handbook of Economic Organization: Integrating Economic and Organization Theory* (pp. 355–382). Cheltenham: Edward Elgar Publishing.

Lapierre, J. (1997). What does value mean in business-to-business professional services? *International Journal of Service Industry Management, 8*(5), 377–397. https://doi.org/10.1108/09564239710189817

Lapierre, J. (2000). Customer-perceived value in industrial contexts. *Journal of Business & Industrial Marketing, 15*(2/3), 122–145. https://doi.org/10.1108/08858620010316831

Leonard-Barton, D. (1991). Inanimate Integrators: A Block of Wood Speaks. *Design Management Journal, 2*(3), 61–67. https://doi.org/10.1111/j.1948-7169.1991.tb00579.x

Leseure, M. (2015). Trust in manufacturing engineering project systems: An evolutionary perspective. *Journal of Manufacturing Technology Management, 26*(7), 1013–1030. https://doi.org/10.1108/JMTM-03-2013-0027

Leseure, M. J., Bauer, J., Birdi, K., Neely, A., & Denyer, D. (2004). Adoption of promising practices: A systematic review of the evidence. *International Journal of Management Reviews*, *5-6*(3-4), 169–190. https://doi.org/10.1111/j.1460-8545.2004.00102.x

Levitt, T. (1960). Marketing Myopia. *Harvard Business Review*, *38*(4), 24–47.

Liechty, J., Ramaswamy, V., & Cohen, S. H. (2001). Choice Menus for Mass Customization: An Experimental Approach for Analyzing Customer Demand with an Application to a Web-Based Information Service. *Journal of Marketing Research*, *38*(2), 183–196.

Lin, M. J., & Huang, C. (2013). The impact of customer participation on NPD performance: The mediating role of inter-organisation relationship. *Journal of Business & Industrial Marketing*, *28*(1), 3–15. https://doi.org/10.1108/08858621311285679

Lincoln, Y. S., & Guba, E. G. (1985). *Naturalistic inquiry* (3. print). Beverly Hills Calif. u.a.: Sage Publ.

Lindgreen, A., Antioco, M., Palmer, R., & van Heesch, T. (2009). High-tech, innovative products: Identifying and meeting business customers' value needs. *Journal of Business & Industrial Marketing*, *24*(3/4), 182–197. https://doi.org/10.1108/08858620910939732

Lovelock, C. H., & Young, R. F. (1979). Look to consumers to increase productivity. *Harvard Business Review*, *57*(3), 168–178.

Lusch, R. F. (2006). Service-dominant logic: reactions, reflections and refinements. *Marketing Theory*, *6*(3), 281–288. https://doi.org/10.1177/1470593106066781

Lynch, J., & Chernatony, L. de. (2007). Winning hearts and minds: business-to-business branding and the role of the salesperson. *Journal of Marketing Management*, *23*(1-2), 123–135.

Madhavaram, S., & Appan, R. (2010). Developing complex, business-to-business products: Issues and implications. *Management Research Review*, *33*(7), 715–733. https://doi.org/10.1108/01409171011055807

Mahr, D., Lievens, A., & Blazevic, V. (2014). The Value of Customer Cocreated Knowledge during the Innovation Process. *Journal of Product Innovation Management*, *31*(3), 599–615. https://doi.org/10.1111/jpim.12116

Malshe, A., & Friend, S. B. (2018). Initiating value co-creation: Dealing with non-receptive customers. *Journal of the Academy of Marketing Science*, *41*, 15. https://doi.org/10.1007/s11747-018-0577-6

Mason, J. (2002). *Qualitative researching* (2nd ed.). London: Sage Publ.

Merle, A., Chandon, J.-L., Roux, E., & Alizon, F. (2010). Perceived Value of the Mass-Customized Product and Mass Customization Experience for Individual Consumers. *Production and Operations Management*, *19*(5), 503–514. https://doi.org/10.1111/j.1937-5956.2010.01131.x

Mihiotis, A. (2014). Management of Supply Chain: X-to-order Concepts vs Make-to-stock Model. *International Journal of Business Administration*, *5*(3). https://doi.org/10.5430/ijba.v5n3p30

Miles, M. B., Huberman, A. M., & Saldaña, J. (2014). *Qualitative data analysis: A methods sourcebook* (3. ed.). Los Angeles, Calif.: Sage Publ.

Miller, M. (2012). *B2B digital marketing: Using the Web to market directly to businesses*. Indianapolis, Ind.: Que.

Möller, K., & Törrönen, P. (2003). Business suppliers' value creation potential. *Industrial Marketing Management, 32*(2), 109–118. https://doi.org/10.1016/S0019-8501(02)00225-0

Möller, K. (2006). Role of competences in creating customer value: A value-creation logic approach. *Industrial Marketing Management, 35*(8), 913–924. https://doi.org/10.1016/j.indmarman.2006.04.005

Morgan, D. (1997). *Focus Groups as Qualitative Research.* 2455 Teller Road, Thousand Oaks California 91320 United States of America: SAGE Publications, Inc.

Mosig, T., Grafmüller, L. K., & Lehmann, C. (2017). Business Model Patterns of B2B Mass Customizers: The Case of German Textile SMEs. *International Journal of Industrial Engineering and Management, 8*(3), 99–110.

Möslein, K. M. (2013). Open Innovation: Actors, Tools, and Tensions. In A. S. Huff, K. M. Möslein, & R. Reichwald (Eds.), *Leading open innovation* (pp. 69–85). Cambridge, Mass: MIT Press.

Mustak, M., Jaakkola, E., & Halinen, A. (2013). Customer participation and value creation: A systematic review and research implications. *Managing Service Quality: an International Journal, 23*(4), 341–359. https://doi.org/10.1108/MSQ-03-2013-0046

Naik, H. S. (2017). *Simplifying Solution Space: Enabling Non-Expert Users to Innovate and Design with Toolkits. Markt- und Unternehmensentwicklung Markets and Organisations*. Wiesbaden, s.l.: Springer Fachmedien Wiesbaden. Retrieved from http://dx.doi.org/10.1007/978-3-658-18283-0

Nambisan, S., Lyytinen, K., Majchrzak, A., & Song, M. (2017). Digital innovation management: Reinventing innovation management research in a digital world. *MIS Quarterly, 41*(1), 223–238.

Newell, A., & Simon, H. A. (1972). *Human problem solving.* Englewood Cliffs: Prentice-Hall.

Nickerson, J. A., & Zenger, T. R. (2004). A Knowledge-Based Theory of the Firm—The Problem-Solving Perspective. *Organization Science, 15*(6), 617–632. https://doi.org/10.1287/orsc.1040.0093

Nightingale, P. (2000). The product–process–organisation relationship in complex development projects. *Research Policy, 29*(7-8), 913–930. https://doi.org/10.1016/S0048-7333(00)00112-8

Noble, C. (2011). *Clay Christensen's milkshake marketing*: Harvard Business School Working Knowledge.

Nordin, F., & Kowalkowski, C. (2010). Solutions offerings: A critical review and reconceptualisation. *Journal of Service Management, 21*(4), 441–459. https://doi.org/10.1108/09564231011066105

Normann, R., & Ramírez, R. (1993). From value chain to value constellation: designing interactive strategy. *Harvard Business Review, 71*(4), 65–77.

Novak, S., & Eppinger, S. D. (2001). Sourcing By Design: Product Complexity and the Supply Chain. *Management Science, 47*(1), 189–204. https://doi.org/10.1287/mnsc.47.1.189.10662

O'hern, M., & Rindfleisch, A. (2010). Customer co-creation. *Review of Marketing Research*, *6*, 84–106.

Ogawa, S. (1998). Does sticky information affect the locus of innovation? Evidence from the Japanese convenience-store industry. *Research Policy*, *26*(7-8), 777–790. https://doi.org/10.1016/S0048-7333(97)00047-4

Ogawa, S., & Piller, F. T. (2006). Reducing the risks of new product development. *MIT Sloan Management Review*, *47*(2), 65–71.

Olausson, D., & Berggren, C. (2010). Managing uncertain, complex product development in high-tech firms: In search of controlled flexibility. *R&D Management*, *40*(4), 383–399. https://doi.org/10.1111/j.1467-9310.2010.00609.x

Olausson, D., & Berggren, C. (2012). Managing asymmetries in information flows and interaction between R&D, manufacturing, and service in complex product development. *R&D Management*, *42*(4), 342–357. https://doi.org/10.1111/j.1467-9310.2012.00688.x

Olhager, J. (2003). Strategic positioning of the order penetration point. *International Journal of Production Economics*, *85*(3), 319–329. https://doi.org/10.1016/S0925-5273(03)00119-1

Patton, M. Q. (1990). *Qualitative evaluation and research methods* (2. ed.). Newbury Park Calif. u.a.: Sage Publ.

Payne, A. F., Storbacka, K., & Frow, P. (2008). Managing the co-creation of value. *Journal of the Academy of Marketing Science*, *36*(1), 83–96. https://doi.org/10.1007/s11747-007-0070-0

Peffers, K., & Tuunanen, T. (2007). A Design Science Research Methodology for Information Systems Research. *Journal of Management Information Systems*, *24*(3), 45–77. https://doi.org/10.2753/MIS0742-1222240302

Perks, H., Gruber, T., & Edvardsson, B. (2012). Co-creation in Radical Service Innovation: A Systematic Analysis of Microlevel Processes. *Journal of Product Innovation Management*, *29*(6), 935–951. https://doi.org/10.1111/j.1540-5885.2012.00971.x

Petri, J., & Jacob, F. (2016). The customer as enabler of value (co)-creation in the solution business. *Industrial Marketing Management*, *56*, 63–72. https://doi.org/10.1016/j.indmarman.2016.03.009

Piller, F., Ihl, C., & Vossen, A. (2010). A Typology of Customer Co-Creation in the Innovation Process. *SSRN Electronic Journal*. Advance online publication. https://doi.org/10.2139/ssrn.1732127

Piller, F., Ihl, C., & Vossen, A. (2011). Customer co-creation: Open innovation with customers. In V. Wittke & H. Hanekop (Eds.), *New forms of collaborative innovation and production on the internet: An interdisciplinary perspective* (pp. 31–63). Göttingen: Universitätsverlag Göttingen.

Piller, F., Möslein, K., Ihl, C. C., & Reichwald, R. (2017). *Interaktive Wertschöpfung kompakt: Open Innovation, Individualisierung und neue Formen der Arbeitsteilung. Lehrbuch*. Wiesbaden: Springer Gabler. Retrieved from http://dx.doi.org/10.1007/978-3-658-17514-6

Piller, F., Möslein, K. M., & Stotko, C. M. (2004). Does mass customization pay? An economic approach to evaluate customer integration. *Production Planning & Control*, *15*(4), 435–444. https://doi.org/10.1080/0953728042000238773

Piller, F., Schubert, P., Koch, M., & Möslein, K. (2005). Overcoming Mass Confusion: Collaborative Customer Co-Design in Online Communities. *Journal of Computer-Mediated Communication, 10*(4), 0. https://doi.org/10.1111/j.1083-6101.2005.tb00271.x

Piller, F., Vossen, A., & Ihl, C. (2012). From Social Media to Social Product Development: The Impact of Social Media on Co-Creation of Innovation. *Die Unternehmung, 65*(1), 1–22.

Polanyi, M. (1966). *The tacit dimension*. Gloucester, Massachusetts: Peter Smith.

Prahalad, C. K., & Ramaswamy, V. (2000). Co-opting Customer Competence. *Harvard Business Review, 78*(1), 79–87.

Prahalad, C. K., & Ramaswamy, V. (2002). The co-creation connection. *Strategy and Business*, 50–61.

Prahalad, C. K., & Ramaswamy, V. (2004a). Co-creation experiences: The next practice in value creation. *Journal of Interactive Marketing, 18*(3), 5–14. https://doi.org/10.1002/dir.20015

Prahalad, C. K., & Ramaswamy, V. (2004b). Co-creating unique value with customers. *Strategy & Leadership, 32*(3), 4–9. https://doi.org/10.1108/10878570410699249

Prior, D. D. (2013). Supplier representative activities and customer perceived value in complex industrial solutions. *Industrial Marketing Management, 42*(8), 1192–1201. https://doi.org/10.1016/j.indmarman.2013.03.015

Ramaswamy, V., & Ozcan, K. (2018). What is co-creation? An interactional creation framework and its implications for value creation. *Journal of Business Research, 84*, 196–205. https://doi.org/10.1016/j.jbusres.2017.11.027

Randhawa, K., Wilden, R., & Hohberger, J. (2016). A Bibliometric Review of Open Innovation: Setting a Research Agenda. *Journal of Product Innovation Management, 33*(6), 750–772. https://doi.org/10.1111/jpim.12312

Rassmann, P., & Grafmüller, L. K. (2018). Exploring Drivers and Barriers for Sustainable Use of Resources: The Case of High-Tech Mass Customizers in the German Textile Industry. In S. Hankammer, K. Nielsen, F. T. Piller, G. Schuh, & Wang Ning (Eds.), *CUSTOMIZATION 4.0* (pp. 301–313). [S.l.]: Springer International Publishing.

Reichwald, R., Möslein, K., Sachenbacher, H., Englberger, H., & Oldenburg, S. (1998). *Telekooperation - Verteilte Arbeits- und Organisationsformen* (1st ed.). Berlin, Heidelberg: Springer Berlin Heidelberg.

Reichwald, R., & Piller, F. (2006). *Interaktive Wertschöpfung: Open Innovation, Individualisierung und neue Formen der Arbeitsteilung* (1st ed.). Wiesbaden: Betriebswirtschaftlicher Verlag Dr. Th. Gabler | GWV Fachverlage GmbH Wiesbaden. Retrieved from http://dx.doi.org/10.1007/978-3-8349-9230-7

Reichwald, R., & Piller, F. (2009). *Interaktive Wertschöpfung: Open Innovation, Individualisierung und neue Formen der Arbeitsteilung* (2., vollständig überarbeitete und erweiterte Auflage). Wiesbaden: Gabler Verlag / GWV Fachverlage GmbH, Wiesbaden.

Rice, R. E. (1992). Task Analyzability, Use of New Media, and Effectiveness: A Multi-Site Exploration of Media Richness. *Organization Science*, *3*(4), 475–500. https://doi.org/10.1287/orsc.3.4.475

Richter, U. (2007). *Perspektiven der ostdeutschen Textilindustrie-Grundrisse einer arbeitsorientierten Branchenstrategie*. Frankfurt am Main.

Roberts, D., Hughes, M., & Kertbo, K. (2014). Exploring consumers' motivations to engage in innovation through co-creation activities. *European Journal of Marketing*, *48*(1/2), 147–169. https://doi.org/10.1108/EJM-12-2010-0637

Salomonson, N., Åberg, A., & Allwood, J. (2012). Communicative skills that support value creation: A study of B2B interactions between customers and customer service representatives. *Industrial Marketing Management*, *41*(1), 145–155. https://doi.org/10.1016/j.indmarman.2011.11.021

Sanders, E. B.-N., & Stappers, P. J. (2008). Co-creation and the new landscapes of design. *CoDesign*, *4*(1), 5–18. https://doi.org/10.1080/15710880701875068

Schreier, M. (2006). The value increment of mass-customized products: an empirical assessment. *Journal of Consumer Behaviour*, *5*(4), 317–327. https://doi.org/10.1002/cb.183

Shen, W., & Liu, S. (2003). Formalization, Testing and Execution of a Use Case Diagram. In G. Goos, J. Hartmanis, J. van Leeuwen, J. S. Dong, & J. Woodcock (Eds.), *Lecture Notes in Computer Science. Formal Methods and Software Engineering* (Vol. 2885, pp. 68–85). Berlin, Heidelberg: Springer Berlin Heidelberg. https://doi.org/10.1007/978-3-540-39893-6_6

Shenhar, A. J. (1998). From theory to practice: Toward a typology of project-management styles. *IEEE Transactions on Engineering Management*, *45*(1), 33–48. https://doi.org/10.1109/17.658659

Simon, H. A. (1962). The Architecture of Complexity. *Proceedings of the American Philosophical Society*, *106*(6), 467–482.

Simon, H. A. (1973). The structure of ill-structured problems. *Artificial Intelligence*, *4*, 181–202.

Simon, H. A. (1978). Information-Processing Theory of Human Problem Solving. In W. K. Estes (Ed.), *Handbook of Learning and Cognitive Processes* (pp. 271–295). Hillsdale: Psychology Press.

Slywotzky, A. J. (2000). The Age of Choiceboard. *Harvard Business Review*, *78*(1), 40–41.

Solakis, K., Peña-Vinces, J. C., & Lopéz-Bonilla, J. M. (2017). DART model from a customer's perspective: An exploratory study in the hospitality industry of Greece. *Problems and Perspectives in Management*, *15*(si), 537–549. https://doi.org/10.21511/ppm.15(si).2017.07

Spithoven, A., Vanhaverbeke, W., & Roijakkers, N. (2013). Open innovation practices in SMEs and large enterprises. *Small Business Economics*, *41*(3), 537–562. https://doi.org/10.1007/s11187-012-9453-9

Star, S. L. (1989). The structure of ill-structured solutions: boundary objects and heterogeneous distributed problem solving. In M. Huhns & L. Gasser (Eds.), *Readings in Distributed Artificial Intelligence* (pp. 37–54). Menlo Park, CA: Morgan Kaufman.

Stockstrom, C., & Herstatt, C. (2008). Planning and uncertainty in new product development. *R&D Management*, *38*(5), 480–490. https://doi.org/10.1111/j.1467-9310.2008.00532.x

Stoppa, M., & Chiolerio, A. (2014). Wearable electronics and smart textiles: A critical review. *Sensors*, *14*(7), 11957–11992. https://doi.org/10.3390/s140711957

Suh, N. P. (2005). *Complexity: Theory and applications. The MIT-Pappalardo series in mechanical engineering*. Oxford: Oxford University Press.

Taghizadeh, S. K., Jayaraman, K., Ismail, I., & Rahman, S. A. (2016). Scale development and validation for DART model of value co-creation process on innovation strategy. *Journal of Business & Industrial Marketing*, *31*(1), 24–35. https://doi.org/10.1108/JBIM-02-2014-0033

Teirlinck, P. (2018). Pathways for knowledge exchange in SMEs in software-driven knowledge-intensive business services. *R&D Management*, *48*(3), 343–353. https://doi.org/10.1111/radm.12311

Teirlinck, P., & Spithoven, A. (2013). Formal R&D management and strategic decision making in small firms in knowledge-intensive business services. *R&D Management*, *43*(1), 37–51. https://doi.org/10.1111/j.1467-9310.2012.00701.x

Teplov, R., Albats, E., & Podmetina, D. (2018). What does open innovation mean? Business versus academic perceptions. *International Journal of Innovation Management*, *51*(1), 1950002. https://doi.org/10.1142/S1363919619500026

Thallmaier, S. R. (2015). *Customer co-design: A study in the mass customization industry*. HHL Graduate School of Management, Diss.—Leipzig, 2014. *Markt- und Unternehmensentwicklung Markets and Organisations*. Wiesbaden, s.l.: Springer Fachmedien Wiesbaden. Retrieved from http://dx.doi.org/10.1007/978-3-658-07526-2

Thomke, S., & von Hippel, E. (2002). Customers as innovators: a new way to create value. *Harvard Business Review*, *80*(4), 74–85.

Tidd, J., & Bessant, J. (2018). Innovation Management Challenges: From Fads to Fundamentals. *International Journal of Innovation Management*, *22*(5), 1840007. https://doi.org/10.1142/s1363919618400078

Tidd, J., & Bessant, J. R. (2013). *Managing innovation: Integrating technological, market and organizational change* (5. ed.). Chichester: Wiley.

Tracy, S. J. (2010). Qualitative Quality: Eight "Big-Tent" Criteria for Excellent Qualitative Research. *Qualitative Inquiry*, *16*(10), 837–851. https://doi.org/10.1177/1077800410383121

Trischler, J., Pervan, S. J., & Scott, D. R. (2017). Exploring the "black box" of customer co-creation processes. *Journal of Services Marketing*, *31*(3), 265–280. https://doi.org/10.1108/JSM-03-2016-0120

Tuli, K. R., Kohli, A. K., & Bharadwaj, S. G. (2007). Rethinking Customer Solutions: From Product Bundles to Relational Processes. *Journal of Marketing*, *71*(3), 1–17. https://doi.org/10.1509/jmkg.71.3.1

Ulaga, W. (2001). Customer Value in Business Markets: An Agenda for Inquiry. *Industrial Marketing Management*, *30*(4), 315–319. https://doi.org/10.1016/S0019-8501(01)00151-1

Ulaga, W. (2003). Capturing value creation in business relationships: A customer perspective. *Industrial Marketing Management*, *32*(8), 677–693. https://doi.org/10.1016/j.indmarman.2003.06.008

Ulaga, W., & Eggert, A. (2005). Relationship Value in Business Markets: The Construct and Its Dimensions. *Journal of Business-to-Business Marketing*, *12*(1), 73–99. https://doi.org/10.1300/J033v12n01_04

Ullman, D. G. (2010). *The mechanical design process* (4. ed.). *McGraw-Hill series in mechanical engineering*. Boston: McGraw-Hill Higher Education.

Ulrich, K. T., & Eppinger, S. D. (2012). *Product design and development* (5th ed.). New York: McGraw-Hill Irwin.

Usman, M., Roijakkers, N., Vanhaverbeke, W., & Frattini, F. (2018). A Systematic Review of the Literature on Open Innovation in SMEs. In W. Vanhaverbeke (Ed.), *Researching open innovation in SMEs*. New Jersey, New Jersey: World Scientific.

Van de Vrande, V., Jong, J. P. de, Vanhaverbeke, W., & Rochemont, M. de. (2009). Open innovation in SMEs: Trends, motives and management challenges. *Technovation*, *29*(6-7), 423–437. https://doi.org/10.1016/j.technovation.2008.10.001

Van Langenhove, L. (Ed.). (2007). *Smart textiles for medicine and healthcare: Materials, systems and applications. Woodhead publishing in textiles*. Boca Raton, Florida, Cambridge, England, s.l.: CRC Press. Retrieved from http://www.sciencedirect.com/science/book/9781845690274

Vaquero Martín, M., Reinhardt, R., & Gurtner, S. (2016). Stakeholder integration in new product development: A systematic analysis of drivers and firm capabilities. *R&D Management*, *46*(S3), 1095–1112. https://doi.org/10.1111/radm.12220

Vargo, S. L., & Lusch, R. F. (2004). Evolving to a New Dominant Logic for Marketing. *Journal of Marketing*, *68*(1), 1–17. https://doi.org/10.1509/jmkg.68.1.1.24036

Vargo, S. L., & Lusch, R. F. (2008). Service-dominant logic: continuing the evolution. *Journal of the Academy of Marketing Science*, *36*(1), 1–10. https://doi.org/10.1007/s11747-007-0069-6

Vargo, S. L., & Lusch, R. F. (2011). It's all B2B…and beyond: Toward a systems perspective of the market. *Industrial Marketing Management*, *40*(2), 181–187. https://doi.org/10.1016/j.indmarman.2010.06.026

Verschuren, P., & Hartog, R. (2005). Evaluation in Design-Oriented Research. *Quality & Quantity*, *39*(6), 733–762. https://doi.org/10.1007/s11135-005-3150-6

Verworn, B., Herstatt, C., & Nagahira, A. (2008). The fuzzy front end of Japanese new product development projects: Impact on success and differences between incremental and radical projects. *R&D Management*, *38*(1), 1–19. https://doi.org/10.1111/j.1467-9310.2007.00492.x

Von Hippel, E. (1978). A customer-active paradigm for industrial product idea generation. *Research Policy*, *7*(3), 240–266. https://doi.org/10.1016/0048-7333(78)90019-7

Von Hippel, E. (1990a). Task partitioning: An innovation process variable. *Research Policy*, *19*(5), 407–418. https://doi.org/10.1016/0048-7333(90)90049-C

Von Hippel, E. (1990b). *The impact of "sticky" information on innovation and problem-solving*. Working Paper No. BPS 3147-90. Cambridge, Massachusetts.

Von Hippel, E. (1994). "Sticky Information" and the Locus of Problem Solving: Implications for Innovation. *Management Science*, *40*(4), 429–439. https://doi.org/10.1287/mnsc.40.4.429

Von Hippel, E. (2001). User toolkits for innovation. *Journal of Product Innovation Management*, *18*(4), 247–257. https://doi.org/10.1111/1540-5885.1840247

Von Hippel, E. (2005a). *Democratizing innovation*: The MIT Press. Retrieved from http://web.mit.edu/evhippel/www/democ1.htm

Von Hippel, E. (2005b). Democratizing innovation: The evolving phenomenon of user innovation. *Journal Für Betriebswirtschaft*, *55*(1), 63–78. https://doi.org/10.1007/s11301-004-0002-8

Von Hippel, E., & Katz, R. (2002). Shifting Innovation to Users via Toolkits. *Management Science*, *48*(7), 821–833. https://doi.org/10.1287/mnsc.48.7.821.2817

Wei, W. (2012). The impact of product complexity on adoption of web-based interactive innovation practices. *Innovation: Management, Policy & Practice*, *14*(3), 431–445. https://doi.org/10.5172/impp.2012.14.3.431

Wheelwright, S. C., & Clark, K. B. (1994). Accelerating the Design-build-test Cycle for Effective Product Development. *International Marketing Review*, *11*(1), 32–46. https://doi.org/10.1108/02651339410057509

Williamson, O. E. (1981). The Economics of Organization: The Transaction Cost Approach. *American Journal of Sociology*, *87*(3), 548–577. https://doi.org/10.1086/227496

Witell, L., Kristensson, P., Gustafsson, A., & Löfgren, M. (2011). Idea generation: Customer co-creation versus traditional market research techniques. *Journal of Service Management*, *22*(2), 140–159. https://doi.org/10.1108/09564231111124190

Yin, R. K. (2014). *Case study research: Design and methods* (Fifth edition). Los Angeles: SAGE.

Zahay, D., Schultz, D., & Kumar, A. (2015). Reimagining branding for the new B2B digital marketplace. *Journal of Brand Strategy*, *3*(5), 357–372.

Zeithaml, V. A. (1988). Consumer Perceptions of Price, Quality, and Value: A Means-End Model and Synthesis of Evidence. *Journal of Marketing*, *52*(3), 2. https://doi.org/10.2307/1251446

Annexes

L. K. Grafmüller, *Co-Creation of High-Tech Products in the B2B Domain*,
Markt- und Unternehmensentwicklung Markets and Organisations,
https://doi.org/10.1007/978-3-658-28412-1

Annex I: Overview of related publications

This annex encompasses the publications of the author of this dissertation related to and cited in the dissertation. It comprises articles presented at international conferences, journal publications and book chapters. Parts of these articles have been used in this work, in each case indicated in a footnote.

In accordance with the respective co-author, the following articles presented at international conferences constitute the basis for the empirical studies of this dissertation:

- Grafmüller, L. K., & Habicht, H. (2016). The value of mass-customized products. Exploring its peculiarities for business customers. Paper presented at the *7th International Conference on Mass Customization and Personalization in Central Europe*, Novi Sad, Serbia, September 21-23, 2016.
- Grafmüller, L. K., Velamuri, V. K., & Möslein, K. M. (2017). Strategies for value co-creation in complex B2B settings: A provider's perspective. Paper presented at the *XXVIII ISPIM Innovation Conference*, Vienna, Austria, June 18-21, 2017.
- Grafmüller, L. K., Velamuri, V. K., & Möslein, K. M. (2017). Identifyinng strategies for value co-creation in complex B2B settings: A provider's perspective. Paper presented at the *2017 R&D Management Conference,* Leuven, Belgium, July 1-5, 2017.
- Grafmüller, L. K. (2017). A B2B toolkit for complex, customized offerings: Informing the physical co-creation beforehand. Paper presented at *The 2017 World Mass Customization & Personalization Conference*, Aachen, Germany, November 19, 2017.
- Grafmüller, L. K., & Rein H. (2018). How to capture uncomplex customer specifications for complex product co-creation: Designing a toolkit for the B2B context. Paper presented at the *8th International Conference on Mass Customization and Personalization in Central Europe*, Novi Sad, Serbia, September 19-21, 2018.

In all articles, the first author also had the lead for the article conceptualization, data collection, and analysis as well as data interpretation.

In this dissertation, also other publications are quoted to which the author contributed, especially to delineate the domain of the context of this dissertation. This applies to the following articles:

- Gebhardt, R., Grafmüller L. K., Barteld M., & Mosig T. (2016). Mass-customized Technical Textiles - Challenges to the Textile Industry of tomorrow. Paper presented at the *24th International IFATCC Congress*, Pardubice, Czech Republic, June 13-16, 2016.
- Gebhardt, R., Barteld, M., Grafmüller, L. K., Mosig, T., and Weiß, M. (2017). Mass Customized Technical Textiles in the B2B Sector. *IOP Conference Series: Materials Science and Engineering* 254, 152004.
- Grafmüller, L. K., & Habicht, H. (2017). Current Challenges for Mass Customization on B2B Markets. In *Managing Complexity*, J. Bellemare, S. Carrier, K. Nielsen and F. T. Piller, Eds. Springer International Publishing, Cham, 269–279.
- Grafmüller, L. K., & Möslein, K. M. (2017). Customer Co-Creation – Wie aus Kundenwünschen interaktiv ein Produktdesign entsteht. In *Digital vernetzt. Transformation der Wertschöpfung. Szenarien, Optionen und Erfolgsmodelle für smarte Geschäftsmodelle, Produkte und Services*, H.-H. Jung and P. Kraft, Eds. Hanser, München, 57–70.
- Mosig, T., Grafmüller, L. K., & Lehmann, C. (2017). Business Model Patterns of B2B Mass Customizers: The Case of German Textile SMEs. *International Journal of Industrial Engineering and Management* 8, 3, 99–110.
- Rassmann, P. and Grafmüller, L. K. (2018). Exploring Drivers and Barriers for Sustainable Use of Resources: The Case of High-Tech Mass Customizers in the German Textile Industry. In *CUSTOMIZATION 4.0*, S. Hankammer, K. Nielsen, F. T. Piller, G. Schuh and Wang Ning, Eds. Springer International Publishing, 301-313.
- Grafmüller, L. K., Hankammer, S., Hönigsberg, S., & Wache, H. (2018). Developing complex, mass-customized products in SME networks: Perspectives from co-creation, solution space development, and information system design. *International Journal of Industrial Engineering and Management* 9, 4, 215-227.

The dissertation project has, moreover, benefited from valuable feedback from several doctoral colloquia, where the following presentations were held:

- Grafmüller, L. K. (2016). Studies on complex product co-creation. *Doctoral Student Workshop (DSW-2016)* of the *7th International Conference on Mass Customization and Personalization in Central Europe*, Novi Sad, Serbia, September 21, 2016.
- Grafmüller, L. K. (2017). A B2B toolkit for complex, customized offerings: Informing the physical co-creation beforehand. *12th Research Colloquium on "Innovation & Value Creation 2017"*, Hamburg, Germany, November 30-December 2, 2017.
- Grafmüller, L. K. (2017). Co-creation in complex B2B settings. *RADMA 2017 PhD Colloquium,* Leuven, Belgium, July 1-2, 2017.
- Grafmüller, L. K. (2017). Co-creation of complex, customized offerings. *Doctoral Colloquium* of the *The 2017 World Mass Customization & Personalization Conference*, Aachen, Germany, November 19, 2017.
- Grafmüller, L. K. (2018). Co-creation of high-tech products in the B2B domain. *Doctoral Student Workshop (DSW-2018)* at the *8th International Conference on Mass Customization and Personalization in Central Europe*, Novi Sad, Serbia, September 19-21, 2018.

Annex II: Supportive quotes for 2nd order themes interpretations for *Part II*

Dimension	Themes	Representative Quotes
Building an open and trustful relationship	Opening up oneself	Hugo: "We are probably the only ones in Europe who can really handle that technology. So we can open up everything, why not? Others can't copy our know-how anyway."
	Announcing uncertainty within the process	Bert: "We actively push every discrepancy and tell the customer in that case that we cannot make it 100% that he doesn't get disappointed."
Avoiding incorrect specification	Investing in explanation & enabling customers	Bert: "There are tons of options, technologies, designs, fields of application. There's only one thing that really counts: taking time for the customer, explaining the options to him, testing, and helping him." Christian: "Our customers are often hesitant to reveal the final application or their customer. They are afraid we could exploit their ideas. The only thing we can do is open up ourselves and hope the customer does the same thing." Andreas: "Before we meet up I always say: 'The more information you give us in advance, the better your product will be and the faster we'll get to your next generation.' That's what we promise and this almost always works out."
	Investing in understanding the context	Benjamin: "Yes, even I learn in this process. It's deeply explained to me how the customer will use our product. I urge my customer to enable me to capture all the details."
	Integrating various stakeholders throughout the co-creation process	Kerstin: "[By inviting marketing, procurement, technical directors and salespeople] everybody is satisfied, because everybody contributed. Politically, too, this approach helps to shorten processes." Greg: "Actually, we want to speak with the salespeople in the early product development stage, not only with their procurement – they are much better at expressing what they need to succeed with their customers and are typically more open."
Adapting to different customer types	Type I: efficiency-driven customer	Petra: "Lots of difficulties to make them [customers] come to us, they don't want to invest that much time. It's crucial to show that you actually require them to develop the complex product they want." Petra: "We try to read every wish from their eyes and do as much as possible ourselves."
	Type II: design-oriented customer	Tom: "Some [customers] want to be inspired and engaged in development. They get really excited when it comes to joint developing." Benjamin: "Sure they are technical guys, but also they like being creative and to be involved in more creative tasks."
Creating physical spaces	Using boundary objects	Friedrich: "Haptics, plasticity, roughness… you need to feel that. There is nothing like a simulation or measurements that work, so you've always got to hold it in your hand. That helps a lot to reduce uncertainty in the process." Bert: "Nobody would choose from a bunch of samples–and they would increase every day. We must think ahead and show him proper solutions and designs. That's the way."
	Scheduling co-creation hackathons	Andreas: "We hold an 'Innovation Day' where our customer is invited. They come to us. First we quickly check the concept in the office and then we move to the production site to actually produce."

The manufacturer's authorised representative in the EU is Springer Nature Customer Service Centre GmbH, Europaplatz 3, 69115 Heidelberg, Germany. If you have any concerns regarding our products, please contact ProductSafety@springernature.com

Printed and bound by CPI Group (UK) Ltd, Croydon, CR0 4YY
25/09/2026
02222849-0002